THE SCHOOL REVOLUTION

ALSO BY RON PAUL

Liberty Defined

End the Fed

The Revolution: A Manifesto

A Foreign Policy of Freedom:
Peace, Commerce, and Honest Friendship

Pillars of Prosperity: Free Markets,
Honest Money, Private Property

The Case for Gold: A Minority Report
of the United States Gold Commission

THE SCHOOL REVOLUTION

A New Answer for Our Broken Education System

RON PAUL

GRAND CENTRAL
PUBLISHING

NEW YORK   BOSTON

Grand Central Publishing
Hachette Book Group
237 Park Avenue
New York, NY 10017

www.HachetteBookGroup.com

Printed in the United States of America

RRD-C

First Edition: September 2013
10 9 8 7 6 5 4 3 2 1

Grand Central Publishing is a division of Hachette Book Group, Inc.
The Grand Central Publishing name and logo is a trademark of Hachette Book Group, Inc.

The Hachette Speakers Bureau provides a wide range of authors for speaking events. To find out more, go to www.hachettespeakersbureau.com or call (866) 376-6591.

The publisher is not responsible for websites (or their content) that are not owned by the publisher.

Library of Congress Control Number: 2013945222

CONTENTS

My Experience in Public Schools

I am a product of the public school system of a different time. Today's system cannot be compared to the public school I attended in the small town of Green Tree, just outside Pittsburgh, Pennsylvania.

The highest authority in managing my school came from our neighbors who served on the school board. It was a different era. I started in the first grade a few months before Pearl Harbor was bombed. It was the same school system that my dad, my aunts, and my uncles had attended.

There was nothing perfect about it—as I remember, both educational and disciplinary policies came up short—but compared to the average public schools in our cities and towns today, it was safe, drug-free, and with no dropouts.

Both in grade school and high school, I remember there were fights and roughhousing, but never once were the police called.

In twelve years of public education, I do not recall any classmate who came from a broken home—never heard of a friend with divorced parents. Possibly, this was a reflection of the time in which I lived.

One advantage we had then was the size of the school and classes. My eighth-grade class had twenty students—most of whom had been through the entire eight years together.

Each day the Bible was read, the Lord's Prayer was said, and the Pledge of Allegiance was recited. No one objected, mainly because the school atmosphere reflected the values of the local community. The federal government was not yet endowed with the authority to keep us safe from ourselves. That came later to the schools throughout the country, as responsibility moved from local schools to huge school districts, state-government controls, and finally the intrusions of the federal courts and federal bureaucrats. None of this existed back then.

The most aggressive "bending of the rules" I did was sneak out and skip recess or intermission or gym class—a block of time with less supervision. I remember it clearly. I'd have to throw my coat out the window and then walk past a few teachers monitoring the corridors (who might have asked me questions as to why I was wearing a coat). Obviously, supervision of one's coming and going wasn't overly strict. Then I'd grab my bike and hurry home, get my newspapers delivered rapidly, and arrive back at school to fall into place for the next class. My motivation was to be able to stay after school for basketball practice and not have to worry about delivering my papers late in the evening.

While in high school, at the age of fourteen, I worked in

the local drugstore at the handsome wage of thirty-five cents per hour. Looking back, I find it surprising that I sold and could buy cough medicine with codeine without a prescription or parental permission. I never saw one classmate abuse this "dangerous" drug. Sneaking a smoke was the big crime in which kids occasionally engaged.

In the summer, I worked for the school, painting, scrubbing, and cleaning. It was hard work, starting at 7:00 A.M., but I was paid more than the thirty-five cents an hour I got at the drugstore.

In grade school, math was my best subject. All twenty of us in class got the same assignment: a list of problems to do and have checked individually by the teacher. Once the given problems were completed, we were allowed to loaf. The sooner I finished, the longer I could loaf while waiting for everyone to catch up, all the while probably making noise and interrupting the others. It was a game for me, and it wasn't until much later that I realized it would have been better for the school to adapt the teaching scenario to each student's ability—something now well understood in homeschooling. Progressing at one's own pace certainly makes sense.

Even for this small town, graduation from elementary school was a big deal, complete with gowns and a fancy ceremony.

High school required traveling a few miles to the neighboring town of Dormont, since our population couldn't support grades nine through twelve. This going next door for high school, an agreement between two towns, was nothing like the giant complexes we see today as a result of local communities losing control over their schools and putting thousands of kids under one roof.

High school, in a similar fashion to grade school, had both good and bad teachers, but compared to today, the atmosphere was rather sedate. I witnessed some drinking, but I never saw any drug use nor was aware of any. Having witnessed a few classmates overindulging in alcohol made me respect—and, in a way, fear—the ill effects of alcohol, and it was for that reason that I didn't touch it in high school or college. This early experience was one of the reasons alcohol had no significant attraction for me. Besides, I never did feel the need to do something just because others were doing it. I enjoyed being different, especially if it made sense to me.

Having a great biology teacher in high school guided me into the sciences in college. I give one particular teacher a lot of credit for my interest in biology and for my eventually getting into the premed program at Gettysburg College.

Running track was a huge event for me in high school, but also a great challenge, since some major knee injuries interfered with my athletic potential. Surgery back then was frequently more damaging than the original injuries. There was no arthroscopic or noninvasive surgery available. My options in track became limited, but later on I found other races to run.

Today, it may not be races to run, but there are plenty of policies to push. This has been a great substitute for me throughout my life.

It was in high school where I met my wife, Carol, who was one grade behind me. She claims she got to know about me was when she was in eighth grade, and watched me run as a freshman in high school. Our first date was on her birthday, when she was sixteen, on February 29, 1952. She chased me, and I finally caught her. We were married five years later, during my last year at Gettysburg.

My high school graduating class had 100 students. For me, small classes seemed always to be best. There were 325 in my class at Gettysburg, and my Duke medical school class was just under 100.

In my early years at Gettysburg, I was undecided about my future. Since I was influenced by my high school biology teacher, I took biology my freshman year because it was a requirement to have taken a science course to earn a BS degree. That was a lucky break for me, as it turned out.

Early on, I thought about teaching biology and about coaching. This led me to start working on a teacher's certificate, since I would need a minor in education. That did not go well. The courses did not make a lot of sense to me—biology did.

In 1956 our education professor, head of the department, was gone for a few days on a trip to Washington, DC, to participate in an important discussion regarding new programs of funding for education. He explained before he left that he was going on the trip with skepticism about government control over funding, but on his return, he told the class that the government had no intention of attaching any strings to funding, and would not interfere with the country's educational process. Washington would be able to help but would never take control. Though I was not political at the time, I recall wondering if that would be the case. The professor was dreaming; my instincts were correct.

Today, one thing is for certain: You cannot compare public education in a small town over fifty years ago to what's happening in these gigantic schools in today's cities, dominated by federal government and federal courts and thousands of bureaucrats and controls and regulations—it's a totally different world.

I've had several members of my family teach in public schools, and some are still involved. Our five children went through the public school system. But with each passing year, it becomes more difficult for me to remain complacent about the opportunities for young children now going to school. Other options ought to be made available to them—all of them. That is why I wrote this book.

THE SCHOOL REVOLUTION

INTRODUCTION

More often than not, we do things a certain way in America strictly because they've already been done that way. Of course, we tinker with policies and institutions here and there, but generally speaking, we don't want to rock the boat too much. The feeling in government seems to be that if something is up and running, ill-conceived though it may be, it should be left by and large intact. The idea of fundamentally altering institutions is almost unthinkable to the powers that run our country. In the case of education—well, we have schools, we have education laws, and we have education policy on the books, so even though the education of youth is one of the most crucial aspects of life and paramount to the future of our country, a real look at the nuts and bolts is never really on the table. But it is for me, and it should be for you, too.

When did this way of thinking begin for me? It was on a Sunday evening in 1971. Richard Nixon went on the air and made an announcement. He said he was suspending the last traces of the gold standard. Beginning immediately, the U.S. government would no longer honor its promise to allow foreign governments and central banks to buy gold from the U.S. Treasury for $35 per ounce. That rule had been in operation ever since 1934. That was the year after Franklin Roosevelt unilaterally confiscated the gold owned by Americans, no matter where they lived. The government paid them $20.67 per ounce. As soon as it had possession of the gold, it hiked the price to $35. That was a windfall profit of 75 percent.

In his suspension of the gold standard, Nixon had not consulted Congress any more than Roosevelt had in 1933. The official justification was this: Such an announcement of a proposed piece of legislation would have led to a run on the remaining gold. While Congress debated, foreign governments and central banks would have demanded payment.

On that same day, Nixon announced full-scale price and wage controls. Again, Congress had not been consulted. He did this on his own authority. He called this declaration "the Challenge of Peace." He announced a "New Economic Policy." Ironically, this was what Lenin had called his fake capitalist reform in 1922, after the Soviet economy collapsed in hyperinflation. Nixon announced, "The time has come for a new economic policy for the United States. Its targets are unemployment, inflation, and international speculation. And this is how we are going to attack those targets."[1]

---

1. Richard Nixon, "Address to the Nation Outlining a New Economic Policy: 'The Challenge of Peace,'" August 15, 1971; see http://tinyurl.com/NixonGold1971.

The next day, Leonard E. Read voiced his opposition to both decisions. Read was the founder of the Foundation for Economic Education, located in Irvington-on-Hudson, New York. FEE began operations in 1946. It was the first free-market "think tank." A decade later, FEE started publishing a monthly magazine, *The Freeman*. For the next two decades, *The Freeman* served as thousands of people's introduction to libertarianism. Read used the word *libertarian*, but he preferred "the freedom philosophy."

Beginning on August 15, 1971, I decided to devote a big chunk of my life to a defense of the freedom philosophy. As part of that defense, I was committed to sound money: a full gold coin standard. My attitude was simple, and it was this: If it is true that we should go back to a gold standard, we should go back to the real one. I believed (and still believe) that the legal right of full gold coin redeemability on demand at a fixed price should be extended to everyone, not just foreign governments and central banks. In this sense, my revolution began in 1971. It is still in full gear. I also argue that legalizing competitive currencies would be big step in the right direction.

My 2008 book, *The Revolution*, was a political one. It was a culmination of the ideas that shaped my 2007 campaign for the Republican Party's nomination for president. The book, while political, was not what is sometimes called a campaign book. By the time I finished it, I sensed I would be dropping out of the race a short time later. I thought of it as a post-campaign book, meant to create new, long-term ways of thinking critically about the issues facing America. Yet it *was* a campaign book in this sense: I hoped it would mobilize Americans on a permanent basis. I raised these issues again in my campaign in 2011 and 2012. I will continue to raise them now that I am out of Congress. I am not out of circulation.

I ended that book's preface with these words:

> If we want to live in a free society, we need to break free from these artificial limitations on free debate and start asking serious questions once again. I am happy that my campaign for the presidency has finally raised some of them. But this is a long-term project that will persist far into the future. These ideas cannot be allowed to die, buried beneath the mind-numbing chorus of empty slogans and inanities that constitute official political discourse in America.
>
> That is why I wrote this book.[2]

My subject was politics. But politics is only one part of my work. Indeed, the freer the society, the smaller the political part is. To limit the work for liberty to politics is to play into the hands of numerous political interest groups with agendas that all boil down to this: social salvation by legislation. I simply do not believe in that agenda.

---

2. Ron Paul, *The Revolution: A Manifesto* (New York: Grand Central Publishing, 2008), p. ix.

I began chapter 5, "Civil Liberties and Personal Freedom," with these words:

> Freedom means not only that our economic activity ought to be free and voluntary, but that government should stay out of our personal affairs as well. In fact, freedom means that we understand liberty as an indivisible whole. Economic freedom and personal liberty are not divisible. How do you plan to exercise your right to free speech if you're not allowed the economic freedom to acquire the supplies necessary to disseminate your views? Likewise, how can we expect to enjoy privacy rights if our property rights are insecure?[3]

Because I see my work for liberty as extending far beyond politics, and because I see that freedom is not divisible, I offer this book as the second phase of the revolution. It is related to politics only in this sense: it would take political action to repeal the bad laws governing education. But long before we can expect a majority of voters to oppose all state and federal aid to local school districts and other interventions, tens of millions of Americans will already have pulled their children out of the local public schools. I'll get into this later.

A free society *acknowledges* that authority over education begins with the family. I am not saying that a free society *grants* that authority. I do not believe that such authority

---

3. Ibid., p. 100.

is delegated by society. But a free society *acknowledges* that families have that authority. To the extent that any society substitutes a source of authority over education other than the family, it departs from liberty.

————•—————

The battle for liberty today is best seen institutionally in the battle over the control of education. It is far more visible than the battle over taxes, for example. The stakes are higher in education than in taxation—future voters are trained in the principles of who should decide on taxes: voting rights, political power, tax rates, interest groups, etc.

The structure of education both reflects and reinforces the content of that education. And like everything else, to find out who is in charge of education, just follow the money. To find out why the structure of authority is the way it is in any school, follow the money. Consistent tax-funded education does not look like family-funded education, just as bureaucratic management does not look like profit management.[4] Whenever the funding of education differs, the structure and content of education differ. Why? Because the system of funding reflects and reinforces rival views about the way the world works, and how it should work.

The social war over education is therefore fundamental to

---

4. Ludwig von Mises, *Bureaucracy* (New Haven, CT: Yale University Press, 1944); see http://bit.ly/MisesBUR.

the future of society. This may not be clear on every battle-field, let alone in every skirmish. But always, in the end, the contending social and political forces collide. There can be no permanent peace here. At best, there can be cease-fires.

In this book, I present a libertarian view of education, from kindergarten through high school and college. This is a major social arena, where rival views are at war. I am calling you to commit to one side or the other.

I will make the case that liberty in education is basic to liberty in every other area of life. I will also make the point that the free market provides a wide variety of educational options. This diversity is now being multiplied through revolutionary digital technology. Technology does two things. First, it cuts costs. Second, by cutting costs, it widens the market. As Adam Smith wrote in chapter 3 of *The Wealth of Nations* (1776), "The division of labor is limited by the extent of the market." Through price competition on a scale never before seen, the Internet is extending the market for private education.

Those of us who believe in diversity—free-market diversity, not politically correct diversity—rejoice in the Internet. We can see the future of liberty here. The future will be far more diverse, and competition in formal education will be part of this diversity. Formal education will be vastly cheaper than it is today, and also vastly superior.

Defenders of liberty are going to win this fight. Technology is on our side. The free market is on our side. The potential for dramatically falling costs is on our side.

I am inviting you to join the winning side in a battle that

has gone against us for more than 150 years. The tide is turning. Let me show you why.

This book is divided into three parts: "The Centrality of Education," "A Strategy for Educational Reform," and "The Ideal School." This reform project is a long-term one, just as the creation of compulsory state education was a long-term project.

Time is on our side. The state's schools are visibly failing, and most people are not satisfied with them. Yet their costs right now are continually rising. So are local governments' budget deficits. "The more we pay, the worse it gets." This is a basic rule of thumb and can generally be applied to everything run by the state.

Parents send their children to tax-funded schools because they see no cost-effective alternatives. In this book, I will show that there are cost-effective alternatives. One of them is my online curriculum (chapter 11). But there are many others.

So spend some time thinking through what I have decided should be phase two of the revolution: educating and training the next generation of students.

We will win this battle for the minds of men and women. We will win it student by student.

PART I

THE CENTRALITY OF EDUCATION

We are late in a 180-year war. It is a war over who will maintain control of the system of education, beginning at about age six and ending with an academic degree granted by some institution. This degree may be a high school diploma, a college diploma, or a PhD. Formal education is the front line for the future of every nation.

Throughout most of history, parents have been the primary educators. When society was agricultural, neither churches nor the government (federal, state, or local) could extend control over the content and structure of education. Fathers taught their sons, and mothers taught their daughters. While there was always progress, traditional modes of thought prevailed throughout most of history. All this changed around 1800. The enormous growth of productivity and longevity that began in the British Isles and on the Eastern Seaboard of the United States has changed the face of the world. But along with this change has come an enormous expansion of state power. Politicians and bureaucrats assert a degree of authority over education that would have been entirely inconceivable two centuries ago. All over the world, governments have extended control over education, beginning with financing, but not ending there.

The old phrase was "The hand that rocks the cradle rules the world." There was another phrase: "Give me control over the child for the first seven years, and I will make the man." This is often attributed to Ignatius Loyola, founder of the Jesuit Order in the mid-sixteenth century. It is sometimes attributed to other Jesuit leaders. Whoever said it, the idea is clear: the person who shapes the thinking of a young child has an important office. The idea goes back to one of King Solomon's proverbs: "Train up a child in the way he should go: and when he is old, he will not depart from it" (Proverbs 22:6).

———•◦•———

Modern educators are convinced of the truth of these familiar proverbs. They want control over the thinking of children, and they want to reduce the influence of parents. They are thoroughly convinced that there are better ways to educate a child than the traditional ways, and they are determined to be placed in authority over the education of every nation's children. It is now a matter of political power, and the professional educators have succeeded in gaining a near-monopolistic control over the structure and content of education during the first dozen years of school.

This control was resisted by Catholic immigrants in the

second half of the nineteenth century. In the second half of the twentieth century, there was an equally self-conscious movement, generally coming from evangelical Protestants, to remove their children from tax-supported schools. The goal is the same in both cases: *to maintain parental control over the structure and content of education.* Parents want their values inculcated in their children. They recognize that the way to gain this authority is to pay for it, but a private classroom education is extremely expensive. Yet now, because of the technological revolution of the Internet, the cost of educating a child today can be minimal. If the parents homeschool their children, the Internet can provide access to almost everything the parents need to provide an excellent education. This is an unprecedented breakthrough.

The battle for control over education will continue to escalate precisely because of the reduced costs associated with Internet-based education. The old rule of the free market is correct: *when the price of something falls, more of it is demanded.* Regarding homeschooling, as the price of online education continues to fall, the main expenses become the parent's time and trouble. Still, this will make it possible for parents to reestablish control over the content and structure of their children's education. They will be able to offer their children a better education than tax-funded schools can offer. They will be able to transmit their values and beliefs to their children, because they can get help from educational programs that share those values and beliefs. The free market will provide many alternatives for parents, enabling them to pick and choose from among a wide variety of curriculum materials.

Why is education central? It is central because each generation passes on its values, assumptions, and skills to the next generation. Parents are in a position to teach children about what they believe matters most in life, and what is more important than that? Because they are in authority over their children during the first two decades of their children's lives, they can transmit a system of values to them. Ultimately, education is a debate over ethics. What values do the parents hold most dear? These are the values they want their children to adopt. Parents have an idea about the way the world works. They have ideas about what constitutes success and failure in life. They want to transmit these ideas to their children, as well as their own basic moral values. Finally, they want to give their children a head start in life. They want their children to be successful, and this requires that the children be equipped to deal with the many challenges in life, part of which is technical education and part of which are core values and beliefs. The educational system is vital for helping parents impart to their children hope for the future as well as the values and skills required to be successful.

This takes many years of hard work and sacrifice on the part of parents. Parents must work with their children in order to persuade them of the truth of their worldview. Parents need help, and educators supply it. There is a division of intellectual labor. Parents can select educational materials in terms of their presuppositions about what constitutes a good education, and a good life. Parents can go outside the household to gain support from professional educators, who will reinforce the parents' viewpoint.

All this assumes that parents are the legitimate agents in teaching their children. But most modern educators do not assume this. Most educators assume that the parents are not competent to be the sole providers of education. They have been able to persuade the state to enter and control the field of education. They have captured the state with respect to the methodology and content of classroom education. They want access to the children, and they have used the state to gain that access.

———————

All sides in this conflict understand that the future will belong to those teachers who are most influential in shaping children's thinking. Every side wants to be able to frame the great questions of life in such a way that students will behave and think in a particular way. Most important, tax-funded educators reinforce the belief in students that they are under the lifetime authority of the state, and that they should not seriously question that authority. They want students to respect that authority, and finance it. In effect, they want the state to replace the parents in shaping children's lives.

This is why there is a growing battle between parents and the state with respect to education. This is why the revolution of liberty I propose must start with the educating of children. The educational system is at the center of the struggle for the commitment of its graduates.

I propose a different kind of education from that which has prevailed in the United States over the past 180 years. To speak seriously of revolution is necessarily to speak about the first principles of life. These principles historically have been taught by parents, but not over the last 180 years. *This is why the revolution must begin in the family*. It then extends beyond the family. It begins with the education of the children, and then extends beyond the narrow confines of the school. Simply put: *there can be no revolution without a revolution in education*. Any attempt to conduct a revolution apart from educational reform is an exercise in futility. It is also an exercise in coercion. Persuasion begins in the household, and it is reinforced by a systematic program of education. The only alternative to persuasion is coercion.

1

EDUCATING FOR LIBERTY

I f you are reading this, then likely at some point, you became convinced that we have surrendered far too much
power to the state. In every area, the state has asserted authority: in money, in education, in economic affairs and taxation,
in foreign policy, in health care, in housing, and in more than
eighty thousand other new ways—every year![1] Step by step,
the state has encroached on the liberties of free men and
women. Yet this was not done overnight. It was done over
decades and, in some areas, from the early days of the American republic.

But you were not taught this in a tax-funded high school
or college. Instead, you were taught that the expansion of the
state is positive, and that without this expansion into the lives

---

1. The *Federal Register* is published daily by the U.S. Government Printing
   Office. In 2011 it published eighty-three thousand pages of new regulations. Each page had three columns.

Americans, the capitalist system would lead to great inequalities of wealth and massive poverty. You were told that the government under President Franklin Roosevelt saved capitalism from itself. You were also told the United States has necessary military responsibilities around the world, and that American taxpayers must bear the burden of extending the influence of the U.S. government across the face of the globe. And that all this is done in the name of extending liberty to all. Here is the problem: the price of this so-called extension of liberty has been the surrender of individual liberty to the federal government.

The textbooks and curriculum materials dominant in the public schools have maintained this view of American life since at least the end of World War II. This has been the story of modern America as taught in the textbooks. We need a new set of textbooks. Better yet, we need educational materials that are not tied to traditional textbooks at all. New technologies involve video production, interactive education, and low-cost publishing on the Internet. It is now possible to create an alternative curriculum without spending millions of dollars to develop textbooks. A standard textbook may cost as much as $500,000 to produce. This has helped keep conservatives and libertarians from producing systematic teaching materials that would provide a different story of the expansion of the federal government since the end of the American Civil War in 1865.

Let's dig a little deeper. The story of surrendered personal liberty to the federal government is the story of surrendered personal responsibility. *Liberty is inescapably associated with responsibility.* As the government has declared people incapable of becoming responsible for themselves and their families, it has grabbed expanded authority over the lives of all Americans.

Any program of education that is deliberately designed to increase the liberty of individuals must begin with this premise: *as individuals mature, they must accept greater personal responsibility for their actions.* Education or liberty must be geared to persuading people to take greater responsibility in their own lives. As people achieve greater responsibility, they also achieve greater liberty. When they become confident in their ability to exercise responsibility, they are ready to exercise liberty.

The whole system of education from kindergarten through graduate school ought to be geared to equipping students to take greater personal responsibility for their actions. This is the meaning of adulthood, and education is meant to prepare an individual for precisely that. But the modern welfare state is premised on a very different view of maturity. It is premised on the view that individuals are not fully responsible for their actions, and therefore they do not deserve extensive liberty. The welfare state winds up treating adults as if they were children. Just as children are not granted a great deal of liberty of action by their parents, so the modern welfare state constantly expands its authority over the lives of individuals. This restricts their liberty of action. If we do not begin with the principle of education that insists that *education for liberty is education for personal responsibility*, the system of education will not lead to an expansion of liberty, but rather, to its contraction.

Parents know from the beginning that they are training their children to exercise maturity as adults. Parents want their children to be capable adults at some point, and they devote time and energy to helping their children understand the principles of successful living. Their job is to teach their children ethics, both verbally and by example, through their own actions. They teach their children skills that are needed in order to be successful in life. They teach their children habits of behavior, including basic manners, that are essential to success in life. Parents do their best to teach their children how to compete in a highly competitive world, and to do so in a responsible manner. Linking liberty and personal responsibility is central to this.

By the time a child reaches high school, most of his habits are already developed, including study habits. He already sees the world in a particular way. He thinks of cause and effect in a particular way. Then he is introduced to such academic subjects as government, economics, history, literature, science, mathematics, and perhaps even fine arts. All this should be taught from a consistent perspective. All of it should be taught with this in mind: *there can be no extension of liberty without an accompanying extension of personal responsibility*. To teach economics, government, and history apart from this presupposition is to mislead the student. Worse, it is to persuade the student that responsible maturity is not based on an extension of liberty, and therefore that the state is the ultimate authority in life.

We tell our children that when they are adults, they will be able to leave the confines of the family. We tell them that they will be able to exercise liberty of action, without depending on their parents for finances or direct intervention in their lives. We want this for them, and that is the message they want to hear. But the textbooks tell them a completely different story with respect to the expansion of personal responsibility and liberty. Textbooks tell students that the federal government must intervene in the affairs of hundreds of millions of individuals because these individuals are not capable of making their own decisions. They are not capable of negotiating a wage with an employer. They are not capable of saving for their retirement. They are not capable of deciding what kind of health care is best for them, given the limitations of their income. They are not capable of deciding what kind of educational program is best for their children. The textbook version of the welfare state tells the story of the failure of the free market to make available opportunities to large numbers of people, opportunities that involve an increase in personal responsibility, but that also bring with them an increase in personal liberty.

In other words, the story we tell our children with respect to their lives—namely, that as they mature, they will be given greater liberty and greater responsibility—is not the story their textbooks convey to them. There is a reason that conservatives and libertarians refer to the regulatory state as the nanny state. The nanny state can, in many ways, be thought of as an imitation of a family nanny. A nanny is hired by wealthy parents to look after small children because the parents work full time or are otherwise overly occupied and need help. The nanny state functions similarly. Yet the family nanny is dismissed at some point, when the children grow old enough to manage without her. Sadly, there is no way to dismiss the nanny state unless we cut off its funding. It will not go away if the voters consent to funding it. It will continue to intrude in the lives of individuals, as if they were children.

So, educating for liberty requires that we educate by means of a curriculum and a program of education that extend the benefits of both liberty and responsibility to students. As they mature, they must be given greater authority over their own education. Parents sometimes do not want to turn them loose, in exactly the same way politicians and bureaucrats do not want to turn us loose. But a program dedicated to educating students for liberty must be consistent across the board. It must give the offer of greater liberty in response to improved performance. It must also present the story of economics, politics, history, and business from the point of view of the extension of liberty. The student had better understand that his quest to gain personal liberty as an adult should be matched by a willingness by politicians and bureaucrats to reduce their interference in the lives of the citizenry. The student wants liberty, and the price of that liberty is greater personal responsibility. This is manifested in improved performance academically. But if the student wants to continue to extend his zone of authority, which involves liberty of action, he must recognize that the nanny state is a threat to his authority to make his own choices.

Conservatives and libertarians insist that *self-government is the most important form of government.* They maintain that the intrusion of the modern state into the lives of millions of citizens is an attempt to substitute the state for self-government. They are convinced that this will backfire, as bureaucracy expands and free enterprise is restricted. But if self-government is the foundation of liberty, it should also be the foundation of education. Students should be encouraged to learn the techniques of research, analysis, writing, and public speaking. As they mature, they must be ready to step out into the world and begin to change it for the better. *The most meaningful way to improve the world is to free up the creativity of individuals.* These individuals can then find ways of better serving their fellow man. Through market competition, individuals find ways of improving the lives of others. They ask to be paid for having provided such improvement, which is a form of persuasion. The alternative to persuasion is coercion.

Parents need to understand early in the process of educating their children that they must begin to remove themselves from that process. They must show their children the basics of education, and then turn over to them, once they are old enough, the responsibilities of mastering a basic curriculum. Considering children too young to be tasked with such a responsibility is to underestimate them.

The curriculum can and should reflect the viewpoint of the parents. The parents should be in charge of selecting the curriculum, so they exercise authority economically in the marketplace. If parents decide that a particular curriculum is not what the children need, and if enough parents make this decision, market forces will eliminate that curriculum from consideration. This is the basis of liberty in economic affairs, and it is also the basis of liberty in educational affairs.

Most parents understand this with respect to college. They know that they are going to have to turn loose any child who goes off to college. Unfortunately, the parents will also be required to hand over a great deal of money. This is one of the problems of conventional, campus-based college education. The parents surrender almost all authority to the university with respect to the content of education, to the moral behavior on campus, and, usually in the first two years, to the dorm room. Parents have to pay a great deal of money to the university for the privilege of turning their children over to people who probably do not share their view of the way the world works, let alone the way the world ought to work. The parents (or students) are saddled with severe economic responsibility, and at the same time, they surrender direct authority, or rather, they delegate it. This is so common today that hardly anybody gives it a second thought. Yet they ought to give it a second thought—and then a third thought, and a fourth thought. Children go off to college, and either the parents or the students, through financial aid, assume whatever financial burdens come along with that. End of story. There seem to be no other real choices, so we just accept this situation. Most people bemoan this process but never truly question it on a grand scale.

The transition from senior year in high school to freshman

year in college is sometimes as radical as the transition from being single to being married, or the transition that takes place when the first baby is brought home. Some students are prepared to make this transition, but millions are not. They are not prepared emotionally, they are not prepared academically, and they are not prepared in terms of the exercise of personal responsibility. In other words, *they are not trained in the exercise of self-government*, and so all that money and time and effort is largely wasted on individuals who are nowhere near being ready to take advantage of the experience. This is tragic, and it is widespread. It's even more tragic because of this little-known fact: it is possible to earn a bachelor's degree from any of several accredited universities for a total cost of under $15,000—and the education can be just as good. But no one tells parents that these options exist. These options don't feel real in our culture. But they should, because the actual education can be just as good.

A system of educating for liberty must prepare a student to make this transition so that it is not wasted. The earlier the preparation begins, the better. It is possible today for a student in a homeschool or private school environment to take all his university course work. He can graduate with a degree from an accredited college or university at the age of eighteen. Not many students do it, but it is possible, and parents and students should know that it is possible. Students who do this have mastered the basics of academic self-government. Parents cannot succeed in nagging the child into this kind of performance, but if the child is self-motivated and self-governing, this kind of performance is possible.

It is relatively common today for academically advanced students in high school to complete the first two years of college by the time high school graduation day arrives. In the state of Washington, for example, there is a program that lets high school students attend a community college instead of attending high school classes, and the students graduate at eighteen with an associate's degree. They then enter university as juniors. This saves parents anywhere from $20,000 to $100,000, an unbelievably large amount for most families. If this is considered legitimate by the state of Washington with respect to tax-funded education, why shouldn't parents adopt a similar program for their children that does not require tax funding or that the student even set foot on a campus?

The important principle of educating for liberty is consistency. There should be consistency, for example, with respect to maturity. The educational program should enable the student to become responsible for educating himself within the framework of a specific curriculum. As the child grows, he should become increasingly independent from his parents, so long as he meets the standards of a curriculum the parents have selected. This places great responsibility on parents to decide which curriculum is best for their child. But, as always, here is the principle: *there can be no increase of liberty without a parallel increase in responsibility*. You must always link those two things in your thoughts. If the parents are going to maintain the liberty to select the curriculum for their children, they must become responsible for selecting the right curriculum.

The curriculum must guide the students both directly and indirectly. It must show the students they are capable of advancing in the program without parental nagging. Parents and student must interact with each other, thereby providing mutual support. The content of the curriculum must be consistent with the structure of the program. The content must show that with the expansion of personal responsibility comes an expansion of liberty. It must show that free men are creative, and that economic growth is the result not of state interference, but of personal responsibility, individual entrepreneurship, and the reinvestment of capital. It must present the story of liberty in such a way that the student understands that what is true for him as an individual is true also of society. It must attempt to convince the student that *self-government is the basis of liberty*. This is the fundamental principle of the *content* of the curriculum, but it has to be reinforced by the *structure* of the curriculum.

If parents wish to persuade their children of the truth regarding personal responsibility and personal liberty, they had better choose a curriculum that is consistent with this goal. If the curriculum teaches Keynesian economics, if it reinforces welfare state politics, if it teaches the principle of the autonomous sovereignty of the state, then it undermines the goals of the parents with respect to their children. In other words, the educational program is schizophrenic. Its content teaches a worldview that is inconsistent with the worldview held by the parents and the very structure of the curriculum itself.

The student must become well versed in the principles of liberty, so that when he steps into the voting booth or onto the university campus, he understands the difference between liberty and bondage. The parents owe their children this kind of curriculum *before* they send them off to college. If the children do not understand the difference, they will be subjected to the intellectual meat grinder that modern higher education has become.

——◦——

I'll say it again. The inescapable principle of liberty is that it cannot be separated from responsibility. This principle applies in every area of life. The fact that young children are irresponsible is the basis of parental authority over them. Children do not possess full liberty. Education must be geared to increasing their level of responsibility, little by little, year by year.

There must be consistency in education. This requirement shapes both the structure and content of education. As children take on more responsibility, they must be given more freedom. If this is not done, they may gain nothing from the college experience. Half of those who enroll as freshmen do not graduate. The transition is too much for them.

2

EDUCATING FOR LEADERSHIP

I f we date the appearance of the libertarian movement to the publication of Friedrich Hayek's masterpiece, *The Road to Serfdom*, which was published in 1944, and which I read in medical school, the movement is more than sixty years old. But of course the publication of one book does not constitute a movement. The first libertarian organization to be set up was the Foundation for Economic Education, started by Leonard E. Read in 1946, as I mentioned in the introduction to this book. A decade later FEE began publishing its monthly magazine, *The Freeman*. That magazine became an important recruiting tool for the next three decades. I think it is safe to say that it launched the libertarian movement.

Leonard Read wrote a book in 1962 titled *Elements of Libertarian Leadership*. He begins chapter 1 with this statement:

Almost everyone says he favors freedom; just try to find a single individual who says he does not. The search would almost certainly prove fruitless. Indeed, so many declare themselves for freedom and against communism that hundreds of organizations now exist to satisfy the common devotion to this attractive term. But, in spite of this lip service to freedom, our actual liberties continue to dwindle. The centralized state makes more and more of our decisions for us.[1]

The rest of Read's book is devoted to an explanation for this discontinuity between rhetoric and reality. He blames a lack of leadership, but a very special form of leadership: one based on self-improvement. He goes on to say:

All individuals are faced with the problem of whom to improve, themselves or others. Their aim, it seems to me, should be to effect their own unfolding, the upgrading of their own consciousness, in short, self-perfection. Those who don't even try or, when trying, find self-perfection too difficult, usually seek to expend their energy on others. Their energy has to find some target. Those who succeed in directing their energy inward—particularly if they be blessed with great energy, like Goethe, for instance—become moral leaders. Those who fail to direct their energy inward and let it manifest itself externally—particularly if they be of great energy, like

---

1. Leonard E. Read, *Elements of Libertarian Leadership* (Irvington-on-Hudson, NY: Foundation for Economic Education, 1962), p.13; see http://bit.ly/ReadLead.

Napoleon, for instance—become immoral leaders. Those who refuse to rule themselves are usually bent on ruling others. Those who can rule themselves usually have no interest in ruling others.[2]

I have always taken this advice very seriously. Even though I served in Congress, my goal was always persuasion rather than coercion. My goal was to do what I could to take a stand against the extension of federal government power. I was not successful in getting any piece of legislation passed into law. But I made it clear—to my colleagues, my constituents, and anyone who happened to come across my writings or speeches—that my goal was to do whatever I could to enable others to improve themselves. I favored the restriction of power by the state because I believed, and still believe, that self-improvement, self-discipline, and ultimately self-government make possible a flourishing civilization. I never wavered from that core truth.

I exercised a kind of leadership, but it was not leadership of the masses. It was not leadership based on the mobilization of voters to extend the power of the state. On the contrary, I did what I could to warn my colleagues, my constituents, and anyone else that the United States faced and would continue to face a series of crises precisely *because* the federal government had extended its tentacles into so many aspects of our lives. Whatever influence I have had in American political

---

2. Ibid., p. 68.

life comes from the fact that I did not exercise leadership in terms of the prevailing philosophies of the role of the state. I never recommended trying to capture the state; I recommended shrinking it massively.

Some people may believe that I was unsuccessful in Congress because I did not get legislation passed into law. But libertarian leadership is not based on political influence. Conservatives know the phrase "Ideas have consequences." That is also the title of a book by Richard Weaver from a generation ago. I believe the title is correct. People who want long-term influence would be wise to cultivate ideas that will have consequences. I viewed my role in Congress as being a representative of those ideas—one of which was this one: free people are more creative than unfree people. It has a corollary: if you want creativity to flourish, you must reduce the influence of the state.

I believe that all education should be education for leadership. Leonard Read was correct in his focus on self-improvement as the foundation of leadership.

Libertarian leadership is not about standing in front of a large crowd in order to mobilize them for action; at least, it is not usually about this. Sometimes you may get an opportunity to do something like that, and I have been able to stand in front of thousands of college students to present the case for liberty. But that came only after decades of critical thinking about the principles of liberty, thinking about ways those principles could be applied, and making speeches in front of my congressional colleagues—which usually failed to persuade them to vote the way I was voting. But here's the truth: The important thing is not to get an opportunity to stand in front of fifteen thousand people and attempt to call them to action. The important thing is to understand the principles of what Leonard Read called *the freedom philosophy*, and to be able to explain them clearly to yourself and somebody else. The essence of leadership is not the mobilization of large numbers of people. The essence of leadership is self-mobilization and self-government and, out of this, opportunities to explain to others why you believe what you believe. If people are persuaded that you are reliable and that you stick to the principles you say you believe in no matter what, they are far more likely to listen to what you have to say. Leadership is more often the case of one-on-one discussion than it is standing in front of a crowd and giving a speech.

Think of your own situation. Maybe you do not want to be a leader, but you are convinced that the principles of liberty are practical. You are also convinced that, when they are implemented, person by person, the world is better off. You understand that creativity flourishes in a society that lets people alone, leaving them to face the responsibilities and wonders and hardships of life on their own terms, to work to overcome obstacles on their own or with their circle of friends and family. You believe, in other words, in the idea of personal liberty. You would like to be able to explain these principles so that people you know will understand them and adopt them. You spend time reading. You spend time thinking about these principles. You begin to develop the ability to articulate these principles in a way that others can understand.

Well, you have become a leader, even though your intent was not to become a leader. You merely wanted to improve your ability to express what you believed in, but in doing so, you inevitably became a leader.

Consistent living draws attention to itself, even though the person who is living consistently does not proclaim this from a soapbox. It is the consistency of a person's lifestyle that impresses other people. We have all heard the phrase "walk the talk." It is an accurate one.

———— ·•· ————

I have been working on a curriculum for high school students that is designed to help them understand the freedom philosophy, and will enable them to articulate it. This involves the ability to read carefully, analyze arguments, write clearly, and defend their position verbally. I am convinced young people have a desire to find fundamental principles of living to stick to and hold as their own, and to conform their lives to those principles. In other words, I really do believe in youthful idealism. I think we should understand and work with this characteristic of young people. They want to be successful in life, but they also want to be successful in terms of meaningful moral principles. They want to commit to something. I am firmly convinced that the reason I have been successful in attracting young people is because they understand that I am committed to a philosophy of life that is deserving of commitment philosophically, but is also highly practical in terms of allowing creative people to follow their dreams and reap the rewards of their efforts. *The freedom philosophy is both idealistic and practical.* This is why it has, and has always had, such great appeal among young people.

One of the reasons that then-candidate Obama attracted so many young people during his campaign in 2008 was because he came in the name of idealism. He came in the name of hope. Both of these are legitimate appeals. Both carry a lot of weight with young people. I never doubted the sincerity of his idealism. What I doubted was the practicality of a philosophy of government that presented the state as an agency of healing. I have no doubt that the philosophy of state intervention is idealistic, but it is deeply wrong as well as impractical. I do not think that implementing a welfare state will produce the results that idealistic young people believe or hope it will produce. The expansion of state power into the lives of individuals inevitably leads to an expansion of bureaucracy. The bureaucratization of modern life is a blight on the soul of men and a straitjacket on their productivity.

It is not good enough to be idealistic. Idealism must rest on a system of cause and effect that will produce the results that idealists seek. If the outcome of a particular form of idealism is the opposite of what the idealist has proclaimed as a major goal of humanity, then the idealist is misinformed. He might come in the name of the high moral ground, but the results of his philosophy undermine that high moral ground. This is why the basis of libertarian leadership is always grounded in a system of cause and effect that rewards productivity, as assessed by customers, and promotes voluntary transactions and associations. It also rests on the principle of peace. The good life is fostered by individuals who pursue their goals in life on a peaceful basis, and who are willing to bear the responsibility for their actions. This is the libertarian principle of *nonintervention*. It means nonintervention by the state. It applies to domestic policy and to the national government's foreign policy.

You may not be young anymore. Or you may be a teenager. Maybe you are in between, or older. My point is this: Leadership is not a matter of age. It is a matter of commitment. It is a matter of being able to understand the freedom philosophy and apply it to specific cases both in theory and practice. If you can understand cause and effect in the world of voluntary exchange, and if you can express clearly this system of cause and effect, you have what it takes to be a leader. Your continued program of self-education and self-improvement is a process of education for liberty.

I realize that I keep coming back to the issue of self-improvement. That was Leonard Read's point back in 1962. It is this principle: *reforming the world begins with reforming ourselves.* If we want other people to believe we are serious, they must be able to see consistency in our lives. Otherwise, they will not be impressed and will not take us seriously. This is why libertarian leadership is so difficult. Jesus spoke about this principle. He said that we must remove the plank in our own eye before we are capable of removing the sliver in somebody else's eye (Matthew 7:3).

One of the best programs of self-improvement anywhere in the world is Alcoholics Anonymous. People who suffer from alcoholism can overcome it through a program of self-discipline and self-improvement. Part of this program involves bringing the message of sobriety to other people who suffer from alcoholism. The simple act of carrying the message is beneficial for the alcoholic himself. The program is based on multiple goals. The main goal is a desire to become sober and stay sober. Part of this program involves helping others achieve the same goal. At the heart of the program is the lifestyle of the person bringing the message of sobriety. He has been able to stay sober for a period of time, which offers hope to the person suffering from alcoholism and who wants to get sober and stay sober. If the person bringing the message continually falls off the wagon and is incapable of sticking with the program, the person receiving the message will find it more difficult to believe it and implement it.

There is nothing remarkable about the methodology of this program, in the sense that there is nothing remarkable about the motivation and the message. But the results are remarkable. Here is an organization that accepts no money from the state, that does not put anybody on salary except specialists who are not members, and that rests entirely on the principle of voluntarism. Every member of Alcoholics Anonymous is expected to become a leader, to get a sponsor and sponsees. Yet he is also expected to remain anonymous. A member is not encouraged to build a large following. A member simply builds a personal following, and this following rests on a system of recruitment that rules out the attainment of power of any kind. It is all done by example. As they say in AA, it is a program of attraction rather than promotion. It is enormously successful precisely because there is no way for anybody in the organization to achieve personal influence and power outside the narrowly focused activity of attaining sobriety and bringing hope to others suffering from alcoholism. I can think of no more libertarian program than this one.

In the leadership training program I have been developing, I emphasize the following skills. First, the ability to think critically. Second, the willingness to act responsibly, taking full responsibility for your own actions. Third, a prospective leader needs to know the basics of communication. This certainly involves writing. It also involves public speaking. Fourth is a system of exercises that help a person develop real competence. Competence is important for step five: self-confidence. Someone who is not self-confident about what he believes in, or also about his ability to improve his life in terms of what he believes in, will have a difficult time persuading others of the reality and legitimacy of his worldview. Sixth is integrity. There can be no successful leadership if there is no followership, and there will not be followership in the libertarian sense if the followers do not trust the honesty of the leader. In a system of political power, it is possible to gain followers by offering to share power, even though the person making the offer is understood to be dishonest. That does not work for libertarian leadership. *Integrity is fundamental because trust is fundamental.* Trust is granted by the followers to the leader. It can be revoked at any time.

In other words, *at the center of leadership is ethics.* Followers are patient with a leader who is not super competent if they are convinced that the person is reliable ethically. Trust is central to all leadership. At some point, the person must display competence. But competence in the sense of mastery of a set of skills is far less important than integrity. The earlier people learn this in life, the more successful they will be. Once again, this principle relies on self-government. If the leader must depend on someone else to whip him into line, he is not a libertarian. He may have the ability to lead others, but he does not have the ability to lead others in terms of the principles of the freedom philosophy.

I am convinced that the freedom philosophy attracts idealistic people who have a desire to make the world a better place. They have this desire in the same way a member of Alcoholics Anonymous has the desire to make his life better and, through that action alone, make the world a better place. He is not looking to whip others into line. He wants to lead by example. This is what we might call *word and deed* leadership. It is leadership that walks the talk.

———•———

So, successful leadership begins with self-government. It is extended through successful followership. A person learns the basics of leadership by working closely with a competent leader who serves as a model. He gains access to the leader through his willingness to submit to leadership. This is the principle of bottom-up leadership. It begins at the bottom. Then, over a period of time, the follower advances in his level of responsibility. Maybe he attends a meeting on a regular basis; he shows up. This is basic and absolutely necessary to success in life, because a lot of people do not show up. Maybe he gets there early. He helps to set up the chairs. He learns how to make the coffee. He offers himself as a servant to whoever is running the meeting. *He becomes useful to somebody else.* As I said earlier, this is the essence of Alcoholic Anonymous, but it's also the essence of libertarian leadership.

When individuals are committed to a program of self-improvement in terms of a philosophy of personal responsibility and voluntary action, they become leaders. This may be in spite of themselves. So few people are faithful servants that those people inevitably rise in the chain of command, even if there is no official chain of command. So few people are reliable followers that leaders reach out to them, train them, disciple them, and put them in positions of leadership.

The program I've developed to teach these principles is aimed primarily at teenagers, but I see no reason older people would not benefit greatly from it. Teenagers have to start at the bottom, the best place to start.

If you are interested in finding out about this program, send an e-mail to:

leadershipcourse@aweber.com

3

EDUCATING FOR LEGACY

M ost people want to leave a positive legacy. Even graffiti artists who spray-paint walls want to be
remembered for something. Today, as never before in history,
it is possible for almost anyone to leave a legacy. You can start
a blog free of charge and publish your opinions. It will probably stay up for a hundred years or more. You can use an
inexpensive pocket camera or your cell phone to shoot a
video and post it free of charge on YouTube. It will also likely
be there in one hundred years or more. It might be there forever. Search engines will let people find whatever you have
said or written. If you have something to say, you can have it
there for all the world to see. This is simply tremendous. It is
truly unprecedented.

These days, most high school students are way ahead of
the rest of us when it comes to anything digital. They communicate with one another with technologies that the rest of
us barely understand. I am positive that I do not have any

thing to tell them they don't already know when it comes to digital communications. But it takes more than familiarity or even expertise with technical matters to leave a legacy. The most important thing is having something important to say. It is my goal to train thousands of future libertarian activists who will dedicate themselves to spreading the message of liberty.

When I say activists, I do not necessarily mean political activists. Other forms of activism are far more important than political activism. There are so many ways for people to make a contribution to society besides politics that it is probably a waste of time for most people to devote time to political activism at all. Each person ought to find some area of life in which he can make a contribution, and then devote himself to making that contribution. So much needs to be done, and there are so many talented people who have the innate ability to get things done, that it is a shame that more people do not become activists. I believe in voluntarism as a philosophy of life, and therefore I believe in volunteering. People always need help. Anything we can do to help one another, either for profit or not, is a contribution we ought to be making.

My goal is to help young people find ways of becoming volunteers. I would like to give them the vision—meaning the motivation—to find their niche in life, and find it early. I don't mean necessarily their employment niche, though that is good, too. I mean their service niche. The earlier a person can find this, the more fulfilling his life will be.

There is a lot of confusion over what is sometimes called a vocation. Usually when people speak of their vocation, they mean their job. When I use the word *vocation*, I have in mind the older usage, which used to be known as a "calling." I distinguish between a person's job and his calling. Put differently, I distinguish between his occupation and his vocation. A job is work that someone does to earn a living. It's what puts food on the table. A calling is very different in most cases. *A calling is the most important thing you can do in which you would be most difficult to replace.* There are a few people who are fortunate enough to find a job that is also their calling. Teachers and preachers are paid to do the most important thing they can do, and for which they would be most difficult to replace. Professional athletes probably qualify as people whose jobs are their callings. So do physicians. There are others, of course, but for most people, this is not the case.

Consider my career. Up until 1976, my career was my occupation, and my occupation was my vocation. I believed that the most important thing I could do, for which I would be most difficult to replace, was to deliver babies. I had been trained to do this. I was well paid to do this. People understood what I did for a living, and I think most people respected my occupation. Most people like babies, so anybody who can help mothers deliver babies has a good reputation. I was content to deliver a lot of babies.

Then, in August 1971, President Nixon unilaterally abolished the last traces of the gold standard. I became concerned that we were going to enter a period of serious inflation. I saw this as a betrayal of the American people, and I believed that it would lead to highly negative consequences. I decided to speak out against this policy, and this led to my decision to run for Congress in 1976. I was elected.

All of a sudden I had a new career. I had a new job. I had a new calling. I guess you would say it was a calling. The trouble, as I found out in November of 1976, was that I was easy to replace. Out of about 180,000 votes, I lost the election by fewer than 300. So I went back to delivering babies. But I had a major decision to make. Should I continue to campaign or should I forget about politics? I decided to continue to campaign, and in 1978, I defeated the man who had defeated me in 1976. I stayed in Congress until 1985. In 1984, I ran for the Republican Party's nomination for the U.S. Senate in Texas, and I was defeated. I went back to delivering babies. In 1988, I ran for president as the Libertarian nominee, then I went back to delivering babies. Then, in 1996, I decided to run for Congress again, and I was elected. You can see my dilemma. I believed that it was important to deliver babies, but I also believed that I could make a contribution to the cause of liberty by using my position in the House of Representatives to set forth principles of liberty, and then to vote in terms of those principles. In this respect, I believed that this was the most important thing I could do for which I would be most difficult to replace.

When I decided to run for the Republican Party's nomination for president in 2007, I believed that this was part of my calling. I ran for the nomination in 2011 for the same reason. I believed that I could get out the message of liberty to far more people as a candidate for president than I could as a congressman working in the shadows. You are probably reading this book because of my decisions in 2007 and 2011 to run for president.

I am involved in a lot of activities today that I hope will leave a legacy. One of them is to create a homeschool curriculum. I also speak out on various economic and political issues. I do this in order to make clear the principles of liberty and their application. It is my goal to persuade thousands of people to make a similar study of liberty and to speak out effectively in their own areas of authority. My recent activities are part of my calling. They are more important than being reelected to Congress. In other words, the most important things I could do, for which I would be most difficult to replace, lie outside Congress. So, I changed my job, but I did not change my calling. My calling is still the same: to articulate the principles of liberty, and to help people see ways in which those principles can be applied in the real world.

———

You could say that I came to my calling somewhat late, but the earlier in life that somebody discovers his calling, the earlier he can dedicate himself to a long-term program of self-education. This should eventually lead to a long-term program of educating others. But, as I wrote in the preceding chapter, education is mainly about self-education. So is reform.

If a student discovers in high school what he should commit himself to as part of his calling, he can achieve more in the long run than if he discovers it twenty or thirty years later. It is like beginning a savings program. The sooner you begin, the sooner the capital growth begins. The longer the compound growth process continues, the larger the legacy at the end of your life. This applies not only to money but also to almost everything we do.

We all know about the fast-changing job market. Very few people find themselves working in jobs ten years after college that are in any way related to what they majored in while in college. It is common for young people to have half a dozen different jobs after college graduation, before they finally settle down in what is anything like a lifetime occupation. The pace of change is incredibly fast, so anybody who concentrates in college on a particular career is probably going to be disappointed. Maybe this will work if he is preparing for a specialty position in a profession such as medicine or accounting or chemical engineering, but if he majors in the general liberal arts, his college degree will likely have very little to do with what he does for a living a decade after he graduates.

Then there is this problem: Half the students who enroll in college fail to graduate. Of those who do graduate, most take almost five years to earn their degrees. This investment of time and money is high risk. If I can persuade high school students to focus on a calling in life, and to regard their occupations as flexible, I will help them to leave a long-term legacy. Getting a good job is a wonderful thing; it helps people put food on the table. But, in the long run, very few people can leave a major legacy based on what they do for a living. However, if they concentrate on some area of service to others in which they are important contributors in the broadest sense, they will be better able to make judgments about what they should do for a living. They should view their occupations in terms of their vocations. They should view their jobs in terms of their callings. The two concepts play off each other. They should view temporary employment, even if it lasts for twenty years, as the means by which they make a major contribution that will last a hundred years after they die.

I realize of course that most people will not make a major contribution that will last a hundred years after they die and impact the whole world. But almost anyone can make a contribution that will help somebody a hundred years after they die. They can write something, or make a video of something, or show someone how to do something. Those little things are meaningful. In today's digital world, people can come across information and put it to effective use in their lives even though the person who created that information has been dead and gone for many years. As I said, nothing like this has ever happened in history. My goal is to help teenagers begin to take advantage of this tremendous opportunity.

If a young person recognizes his calling early enough, he can concentrate on it for decades. He will become incredibly good at what he does. Some researchers have said that a person can become competent in a field with about a thousand hours of work. He can become a master of the field in five thousand hours of work. If he has the innate capabilities, it probably takes ten thousand hours, plus training from a specialist who knows the field, to become a virtuoso. Most people cannot become virtuosos, even if they invest ten thousand hours. But if they do have the innate talent, and they spend two hours a day of intense, concentrated effort to improve their talent, after about ten thousand hours they will become virtuosos.[1] What a tragedy it would be for those people not to find their calling until it is too late.

———·•·———

The goal of my online curriculum is to serve the needs of dedicated high school students. If I get enough students to devote themselves to mastering the curriculum, some of them will become masters in the principles of liberty, and a few of them will become virtuosos. They need motivation to do this. They also need to figure out what their calling is. I hope my curriculum will help them do this.

A meaningful legacy involves several generations of dedicated people. Let me give you an example. In 1871 a self-taught economist named Carl Menger had his book published. It was called *Principles of Economics*. With it, Menger made a major intellectual breakthrough. He argued that economic value is based on subjective imputation, not on innate characteristics and not on the value of inputs to produce a product or service. He rejected the labor theory of economic value. He also rejected the cost of production theory

---

1. Malcolm Gladwell, *Outliers: The Story of Success* (New York: Little, Brown, 2008).

of economic value. He offered in its place a subjective theory of value: the value of the object or service is based on the subjective assessments of potential customers or buyers of that product or service.

Menger taught another economist named Eugen von Böhm-Bawerk. He took Menger's idea and applied it systematically in the area of capital theory, which involves a theory of interest rates. Böhm-Bawerk in turn taught Ludwig von Mises. Mises extended the insights of both these men in the area of banking, money, and capital. He made this breakthrough in 1912. Over the next half-century, he developed these ideas. In 1949, Yale University Press published his book *Human Action*. In that book, Mises offers a comprehensive theory of how markets work. His was the first comprehensive theory of the entire market based on a handful of what he called axioms and corollaries. Beginning in that same year, Murray Rothbard began to attend graduate seminars taught by Mises. Rothbard was not enrolled at New York University, but Mises allowed outsiders to attend his seminars. Rothbard attended them for almost twenty years. Mises retired in 1969. Rothbard in turn taught a generation of libertarian activists and free-market economists, though not in a classroom setting. He did it by the power of his writing ability, which was legendary.

Here we see a meaningful legacy in action. It began with Menger. It extended through Böhm-Bawerk to Mises, and from Mises to Rothbard. Each of these men was amazingly gifted. They were all good writers, and Rothbard was the greatest writer among them. The power of these ideas, coupled with the clarity of exposition, made possible the modern academic libertarian movement. Each of them played a special role. Each of them left something behind for the next one to develop. From the publication in 1871 of Menger's *Principles of Economics* to the publication in 1962 of Rothbard's *Man, Economy, and State*, we see an extraordinary development of ideas. Menger had one important idea, but it was crucial. Rothbard had many important ideas. This was a case in which a series of giants stood on each other's shoulders. I had met Mises, who influenced me greatly, but Rothbard was my friend as well as my mentor.

I am not suggesting that I will ever have this kind of effect on people with respect to the power of my ideas. My contribution intellectually is minimal. My legacy involves the combining of job and calling in a public way that has enabled me to communicate the ideas of Austrian economics to millions of people who never heard of Austrian economics. F. A. Hayek once described an intellectual as a person who deals in secondhand ideas. I guess that would qualify everyone in Congress as an intellectual, since they surely do not deal in original ideas. But, in my case, I am promoting the idea that it is possible to take a systematic body of ideas and apply them to real-world situations. If I can get this idea across to a generation of high school students, I believe that a few of them will be able to make major contributions because they have the innate abilities of a Mises or a Rothbard.

Back in 1936, libertarian author Albert J. Nock wrote a chapter in a book. The chapter was titled "Isaiah's Job." In it, he presented the idea of "the remnant." He said that the remnant is out there waiting to commit to ideas they perceive as life changing and world changing. They seek out people who share these ideas. He argued that anyone who attempts to go directly to the remnant, putting pressure on them to commit, will drive them away. They will find other people to represent them, which means that these other people will express their ideas in a unique way. The remnant is essentially invisible to any would-be leader. Nock recommended a program of libertarian leadership. That leadership involves self-improvement.

Never in the history of man has anything been equal to the Internet in enabling people to find others who represent their views and can articulate these views effectively. Search engines are used day and night to find websites and articles that defend a particular outlook. In 1994, none of this existed. Today, it is rapidly changing the world. With the Internet, the remnant is seeking out people who articulate their deepest commitments. Search by search, people are finding other people who represent the ideas they hold dear. None of this was planned. It all seems random. Nock would have said that it is not random, yet to me it truly seems random. We have the phrase "Birds of a feather flock together." Facebook proves this every day. It proves this to something like a billion people.

Technologies change every day. There is no way that a single technology or digital innovation is likely to become dominant, although YouTube certainly qualifies as a candidate. To choose a particular technology as the technology of the future is probably a mistake. On the other hand, to choose certain principles of action, which are ultimately grounded in ethics, involves making decisions about things that are permanent. Principles are unchanging; their application in history is always changing. Principles such as the Golden Rule are permanent. Treat others as you would be treated. Their violation comes in all manner of creative ways. Some people are amazingly skilled at violating principles in new and creative ways. Other people are equally skilled at obeying them in new and creative ways.

The principles of libertarianism, like the principles of religion, teach that, in the long run, good overcomes evil. The productivity of peace-loving, law-abiding individuals is greater than the productivity of violent lawbreakers. If society promotes peace, it promotes creativity in every realm of life. It promotes economic growth. It promotes the eradication of poverty.

A program of reform must have principles that are consistent and that can be applied in the real world. I am not promoting mysticism. I am not promoting a retreat into some kind of monastic order. I am promoting a program of systematic, lifetime education, meaning a program of permanent self-improvement. This is what Leonard E. Read promotes in chapter 2 of *Elements of Libertarian Leadership*.

If someone at the age of fifteen or sixteen gets a vision of what his legacy can be, and he is also taught the skills required to begin to develop this legacy, all it takes is a motivational program to persuade him to commit. Maybe he commits to one agenda for a lifetime. Maybe he commits for only a few years. But he gets started. He gets the compound growth process operating in his life. He begins to learn how to express himself on-screen, which means both writing and speaking. He begins to advance himself along a path of dedication and leadership. That phrase became the title of an important book written by a man who was a major Communist Party leader in Great Britain, Douglas Hyde, who abandoned the party in favor of Christianity in the late 1940s. *Dedication and Leadership* was published in 1966. It is a great little book. But even more important was the little-known book published half a decade earlier: *Dedication and Leadership Techniques*. This was the printed transcript of a seminar Hyde gave to a handful of priests and nuns in 1962. This book is part of my curriculum. It lays out the strategy adopted by the Communists from Lenin to Khrushchev. Hyde did not believe that freedom-loving people should adopt all the techniques, especially those involving blind obedience to the party. But he did believe that the Communists' appeal to youthful idealism was basic to communism's success during the first half of the twentieth century.

Maybe you would like more information on developing your legacy. If so, send an email to:

mymainlegacy@aweber.com

Here are some things to remember from part 1:

The war over the structure and content of K–12 education has been going on for 180 years. This war has escalated since the late 1950s. Little by little, parents are pulling their children out of the tax-funded schools.

The battle rests on a fundamental difference of opinion. The statist educators are committed to this principle: parents are not trained nor competent enough to make decisions about their children's educations. Millions of parents disagree. They have removed their children from the tax-funded schools. This is an act of faith. They have made a major break with the reigning assumption of the welfare state—namely, that the state should have a monopoly over K–12 education.

The reform of education must begin with a reform of ourselves. We must structure our lives in terms of that principle: *there can be no separation between liberty and responsibility*. This applies to individuals. It also applies to institutions. It applies to all schooling. Children must be taught by families and teachers to honor this principle.

When schools are not structured in terms of this principle, they produce what is sometimes called cognitive dissonance. It is the issue "do as I say, not as I do." In other words, the schools teach about freedom and choice and personal liberty but the school's very existence is in opposition to those principles. This never sells well among children or students. People want those in charge to be consistent. They do not want to submit to people who violate their first principles. Without trust, there is no libertarian leadership. Authorities are then forced to rely on sticks rather than carrots to gain compliance.

They do not lead by example. They do not gain voluntary compliance. They get grudging obedience at best.

Here is my position on government: *self-government is vastly better.* It is far more moral. It is much more efficient.

I want to see a continual stream of leaders in every area of life who are committed to this principle of government. That is why I put together the homeschool curriculum that trains young people to become leaders. But the leadership I favor is uniquely libertarian. It was described by Leonard E. Read back in 1962. It begins with this principle: all reform should begin with self-reform. The libertarian leader should seek to become a role model, an example to be imitated. *Persuasion is superior to coercion.* Libertarian leadership is based on that principle. It is essential that a leader walk the talk. He should speak softly and not carry a big stick.

A major goal of all life, which includes all leadership, is to leave behind a positive legacy that should be worth imitating. To do this, a person must distinguish between his job and his calling in life. He should devote a portion of his time and money to his calling: the most important thing he can do and for which he would be most difficult to replace. Yet he will be replaced; death guarantees this. So he should do whatever he can to train successors. This is a fundamental aspect of leadership.

The goal should be compound growth in this legacy, before a person dies and afterward. This is a long-term legacy: intergenerational. With the Internet, leaving this legacy to future generations has never been cheaper. The technology is here. What is in short supply today is the dedication and leadership necessary to building a legacy and building a following to extend it across borders and through time.

This is what my curriculum is designed to produce: dedication and leadership. But before we get to the specifics, we need to understand the need for educational reform. We also need a strategy. I offer both in part 2.

PART II
A STRATEGY FOR EDUCATIONAL REFORM

There have been calls for reforming the public schools for as long as there have been public schools. Within the educational establishment, there have been innumerable proposals for restructuring public education, in terms of both its curriculum and its methodology. There have been many reforms over the years. Probably the most important one was the substitution of the look-say method of reading instruction for the traditional phonics-based system. The archetype of the system we oldsters remember was Dick and Jane. Dick and Jane had a dog, Spot. For those of us who attended public school in the 1940s, this transition from phonics to look-say is marked in our memories by these phrases: "See Spot run. Run, Spot, run." Spot is not running anymore, except in our memories.

There has been no widely adopted system of public school reform suggested by parents. Every call for reform that has ever been taken up by the public school establishment has come from inside the public school establishment. Every proposed reform that has gained even a little traction in the public schools has been issued from the top down. The centralization of public education has gone on for over a century. The consolidation of school districts, the expansion of the school bus system, and the expansion of state and federal funding in local school districts have all combined to remove parental influence in the day-to-day affairs of the schools. Parental authority may be given lip service by the bureaucracy, and the PTA may officially be consulted (and ignored) on this or that minor local issue, but along with state and federal money has come state and federal control over the content and structure of public education. This is a manifestation of the ancient rule "he who pays the piper calls the tune." There will never be any successful system of reform in any institution that is not accompanied by a change in funding. *The means of reform is always a change in the source of funding.*

The centralization of public education has gone on for so long that, at this point, it would seem to be totally utopian to propose any significant reform. It is not that such reform is inconceivable. It is that such reform is highly unlikely. There would have to be a reestablishment of local funding, local control, and foundational parental input into local education. This would have to be accompanied by the abolition of state and federal funding for education. In other words, the reform of tax-funded education must begin with a reform of the financing of local schools. Any proposed reform of the local public schools that is not accompanied by a call for the abolition of all state and federal funding, as well as all state and federal rules governing local education, is simply utopian. There is no possibility of any such reform. Another ancient slogan is appropriate here: "If you take the king's shilling, you do the king's bidding."

Therefore, any proposed reform of the public schools has to be accompanied by a call either to increase local taxation in order to compensate for the decreased funding from the state and federal governments, or else to adopt drastic cost-cutting. In that scenario, a lot of people would have to be fired. Classes would have to be made much larger. The student-to-teacher ratio would return to what it was in the 1950s, meaning at least thirty students per teacher. This would be resisted by the teachers' union. Of course nobody likes to see people fired. But in exchange for a painful transition, you would essentially wind up with local schools controlled by their communities and the values therein, not by some distant bureaucrat who is pulling the purse strings and therefore calling all the shots.

Furthermore, there would have to be increased reliance on the Internet to deliver classroom lectures into households and distant classrooms. This is already being done across the country—but quietly. This is how school districts are increasing the student-to-teacher ratio—quietly. A teacher who records her classes in digital format can teach fifty students, one hundred students, or even a thousand students, who view the class on a computer screen. Low-paid teaching assistants can grade exams. So can machines and computer programs. This has been done at the college level for two decades. Why not in high schools?

A revolution in funding must be accompanied by a revolution in the content of the public school curriculum. The problem is this: *there is no agreement on the content.* Beginning around 1965—the advent of the counterculture movement—there has been a fragmentation of academic opinion on the appropriate content in the social sciences and humanities. There is agreement only on what should not be taught—namely, anything to do with Christianity. The U.S. Supreme Court has repeatedly decided that no tax funding should go toward the support of any sectarian religious creed.[2] These decisions specifically targeted Christianity. So, now we have a situation in which the bulk of the American population, which is Christian, is taxed to fund the public schools, which by federal court interpretation are not allowed to teach the fundamental doctrines held dear by a majority of the Americans who are paying for the system.

We see a similar hostility to libertarianism. There is no such thing as a public school textbook that favors or even legitimately discusses the historical, political, and economic interpretations of authors such as Ludwig von Mises, F. A. Hayek, and Murray Rothbard. Students at the high school level are taught—as their parents were taught, and their grandparents were taught—that President Franklin Roosevelt saved American capitalism from itself. They are taught to revere Roosevelt's New Deal, both in its interventionist domestic economic policies and its interventionist foreign policy. There

2. http://bit.ly/USSCschools.

is no such thing as a public school textbook critical of the New Deal. There may be a few negative words about Roosevelt's attempt to pack the Supreme Court in 1938, and how Congress resisted this emphatically. That is just about the only mistake Roosevelt supposedly made in his twelve-year career as president of the United States.

So, how can voters reform education in the United States, assuming that a majority of voters want to do this? The tradition of public education, coupled with the centralization of funding by state governments and the federal government, seems to make any such proposed reform a political impossibility.

I have good news. It can be done. There is a working model for such a reform. That particular reform is not yet completed, but it is certainly in its advanced stages. I am referring to the U.S. Postal Service.

———————

For decades, conservatives and libertarians called for the defunding of the post office as a matter of philosophical principle. There were many plans for its abolition. None of them came to fruition. The postal system had a monopoly over the delivery of first-class mail, which is where the majority of profits are. Competitors were prosecuted by the federal government.

Then came what seemed to be a minor revision of the law. The government allowed Federal Express to deliver overnight mail at a very high price. This was not considered to be a direct threat to the post office. It was so expensive to mail packages, or to mail a letter, via FedEx, that the government assumed FedEx would not constitute a rival. FedEx was not prosecuted. Then UPS got in on the act. Year by year, more businesses relied on FedEx and UPS to deliver what, prior to 1971, the year FedEx was founded, would have been called first-class mail.

In 1995, the first graphics interface for the World Wide Web was released to the public. This led to the expansion of e-mail. Year by year, e-mail has eaten into the profits of the U.S. Postal Service. Between package delivery by FedEx and UPS and the effect of e-mail, Facebook, and other social media, the U.S. Postal Service is becoming the equivalent of a dead-letter office. If the Postal Service disappeared completely over the next twelve months, not many people would miss it, other than employees of the Postal Service. The organization is now literally billions of dollars in debt. It is not a free-market institution, and it never was. It was an arm of the government even before the existence of the United States. The British government ran it.

All the calls for privatization of the Postal Service through political action failed. What undermined its monopoly position was the back-door development of expensive overnight mail. No major restructuring of the Postal Service by the federal government was necessary to eliminate it. It has been replaced by better technologies and better services provided by the private sector.

There is an old political slogan: "You can't beat something with nothing." All the calls by conservatives and libertarians to reform the post office fell on deaf ears. The public did not see that there could be any alternative to the post office. Voters could not visualize a world without it. Nevertheless, over the past decade, the post office has steadily faded in importance, yet hardly anybody has noticed. It became an anachronism in full public view. The free market provided alternatives, and people shifted their business to those alternatives without even thinking about the effects this would have on the most ancient government monopoly in the United States.

Here is the most effective system of reform: *voluntary replacement*. It is reform that nobody notices. It is reform that the established monarchs of a government-run system cannot effectively fight. They cannot effectively call the public to defend the entrenched government system when the public barely understands or cares that the system is slowly disappearing.

I propose a comparable reform of the existing system of education. I propose the creation of cost-effective rival educational systems in the private sector. The free market has already begun to do this. Over the next generation, we are going to see the replacement of the existing public school systems, from kindergarten through graduate school. This will not be a result of a systematic program of politics launched by conservatives and libertarians. It will not come as a result of voters going to the polls and electing state and federal representatives who will then follow the wishes of the voters and cut all funding to government education. (To propose this sort of reform is to propose a fantasy. It did not work with the U.S. Postal Service, and it will not work with tax-funded education.)

I propose a strategy that in American football is called the end run. We need an end run around the existing educational system. This end run will come in many forms, but all of them are essentially a single strategy: the replacement of the existing system by educational institutions and programs entirely funded by the private sector. These alternatives will eat away at support for the existing system of government education. Unless local government schools can find ways of competing against a comprehensive array of independently financed private-sector alternatives, they will fail to maintain public support, much like the Postal Service. For the local school districts to do this, they will have to renounce all state and federal funding and thereby renounce state and federal controls. They will have to pull out of regional central school districts. In short, they will have to secede, or opt out.

Hardly anyone outside the federal government is coming to the defense of the U.S. Postal System. There is no mass political movement in favor of restoring its complete monopoly over the delivery of first-class mail. In fact, the public would at this point be widely against that. There is no call to inject billions of dollars of federal money into a bailout of the system. There are no such calls, because the system is no longer vital to the lives of most Americans. They will not come to the defense of something they barely appreciate.

Three developments will reform education: the restoration

of family-based education, the restoration of open competition in education, and the development of educational programs that rely on self-teaching and student-run tutorials. In short, the division of labor in education through decentralization. I explore all three in part 2.

4

FAMILY-BASED EDUCATION

The fundamental principle of education is this: *families have the final say in the content and structure of education for their children.* Parents have ultimate authority institutionally in the field of education until such time as the children reach the age of accountability, which is marked by their decision to pay for their own educations as legal adults. This is an application of the familiar principle I stated earlier: "He who pays the piper calls the tune."

There is only one way that parents can gain authority over the structure and content of education for their children. They must pay for it. Any attempt to transfer the funding of education to some other institution is by necessity a call for the transfer of some authority over that education to that agency. The more that any outside agency funds the system of education, the less influence parents will have in determining the system's content and structure. The federal government tries to get this control with a minimal payment. The day that a school district accepts any federal money, it becomes subject to all the federal regulations. And then, those who pay most of the piper's bills (local taxpayers) call very few of the tunes.

Libertarians are fond of the phrase "there ain't no such thing as a free lunch." Anytime an organization offers to provide something for free, we can be sure this is an attempt on the part of that organization to gain greater control over the institution accepting the funding. Anytime somebody offers something for free, it's time to begin a search for the motivations lying behind the offer of financial support. Take a look at previous results of such funding. Examine closely the increase in responsibility and influence that agents of the source of the funding exercised in the administration of the funds. To quote the famous phrase from the movie *All the President's Men*, "Follow the money."

The principle of parental authority over education is an extension of the principle of parental authority over the lives of their children. Parents bring these children into existence, and they are responsible for their care, feeding, housing, clothing, and training. *There can be no separation of responsibility from authority.* Any attempt to separate responsibility from authority is an attempt to transfer authority to some other agency. Parents inevitably lose authority over the content and structure of their children's education whenever they rely on other institutions to provide funding for that education.

This seems easy to understand, but the vast majority of parents in the West have ignored the implications of the transfer of funding for education to the church or the state. They have ignored the inevitable loss of responsibility that accompanies this transfer of funding. They have therefore also ignored the effects of the transfer of authority over their children's education. They have been content to transfer both responsibility and authority for educating their children. In fact, they have seen it as an advantage that another institution has offered to take over the educational function long associated with the family.

———

It is expensive to raise children. Parents are always looking for ways to cut this expense. Historically, they have resisted the idea that the church or state should actively seek to take over the expense of feeding, housing, and clothing children. Parents have seen this as an admission on their own part of being incapable of providing these services. For generations, there was a stigma associated with taking charitable donations. Men regarded it as a public admission of their failure to exercise responsibility for their families. But this sense of stigma has not been associated with the public funding of education. Parents have surrendered direct control over the content and structure of their children's education, and have even consented to laws that make state-run education mandatory. The combination of compulsory education and the offer of tax money to fund local education proved irresistible. The problem is this: Once the principle was accepted, state and then federal agencies intervened to make the same offer to local school districts that the school districts had made to the voters. They offered to bear an increasing percentage of the financial responsibility of the school systems across the country. Step by step, the centralization of education accompanied the centralization of funding.

Parents have regarded the expense of private schooling as too great to bear, so they have consented to their own removal as advisers in the public school system. There was a time when parents could mobilize and demonstrate at school board meetings. They could get their way because they had control over the ballot box, which in turn offered them control over the purse strings. But, with the transfer of partial responsibility for local school funding to state governments, and then to the federal government, parents lost their influence to shape educational policy at the local level.

What I am proposing is a system of education in which parents regain control over the content and structure of their children's education. They can do so by means of new technology, which makes possible distance learning. In the same way that e-mail replaced first-class mail delivered by the U.S. Postal Service, the Internet has now begun to replace the educational services provided in local school buildings but funded increasingly by state and federal economic grants.

———•◦•———

Parents should understand that they are responsible for the education of their children. They should see it as a moral responsibility. Few parents do, however. This is one of the most important challenges that opponents of the existing system presently face. The technology of the Internet is available to provide quality education to families at low prices or even free of charge. But parents' willingness to adopt this technology has been limited. They do not seem to understand the potential of the technological revolution that has already taken place in the twenty-first century. They have failed to take advantage of the tremendous opportunities for education the Web offers.

Parents worry that they are not capable of teaching their children the basics of reading and writing. The older their children get, the more parents fear they have not been trained to provide a quality education for them. They worry about their own mathematical skills. They worry about their skills in the area of science. They don't know much about the history of Western civilization or even the history of the United States. They have some vague understanding of economics, but they have never taken an economics course that in any way shaped their thinking. In other words, by the time the child is twelve or thirteen years old, his parents are ready to fully hand him over to specialists in education. What they fail to recognize is that far better specialists in education have made available on the Internet teaching materials that students can use to teach themselves, and this material is either free or inexpensive. Of course, parents need to teach the children the self-discipline and responsibility to use those materials. This might not be possible in some cases, but in others, it will.

The fundamental principle here is moral and legal. The fundamental principle is that the parents are responsible for their children, and that they have an obligation to search for specific educational programs that fit the needs of their families. They must make a determination as to which of the programs is best for their children. Sometimes the differences among children suggest that there must be different curriculum materials and educational programs for each child. One size does not fit all. Even within a household, there are sufficient variations in children's capacities and interests that parents must select a wide variety of educational materials. Obviously, I am talking about homeschooling. If the parent wants to pull his children out of the local public school, and he does not adopt homeschooling, then he has to pay for an alternative school. The school probably has athletic fields, buildings, teachers, air-conditioning, administration, and all the other institutional arrangements common to classroom-based education. The private school is an expensive version of the "free" public school, although with variations in terms of educational content. But a school like this must cater to a large number of students, which raises the traditional problem of teachers catering to the lowest common denominator. Also, parents find that they cannot afford private education. They also find that their children may not benefit from this or that course, or this or that curriculum program, any more than they would or wouldn't at a public school.

If parents understood that they are responsible for their children's education in the same way that they are responsible for their feeding, housing, and clothing, we would see far more attention given to the content and structure of educational programs. Parents would seek out the best programs they could afford. They would sacrifice for the sake of their children's education in the same way that they sacrifice for their feeding, housing, and clothing.

———•———

In any call to reform the existing educational system, the cost factor should be front and center. To talk about the need for reform without talking about the cost of reform is meaningless and unrealistic. Libertarians focus on economic costs. When these costs begin to fall, institutional reforms become not merely possible but inevitable. Price competition works its magic. These words change everything, one family at a time: "I can get it for you cheaper, and better."

In any institution there must always be someone who has the final authority to determine the operation of the organization. Money does not come with no strings attached. There are always strings attached. If you follow the money long enough, you find somebody holding a hammer. You find somebody who has the power to say yea or nay to any proposed change in the system. He who pays the piper calls the tune.

With the decline in the cost of homeschooling to levels undreamed of as recently as twenty years ago—with respect to the cost of materials, the campus, and the instructors—parents today are in a position to exercise authority over the content and structure of their children's education. Today, the cost in dollars of educating children has fallen so dramatically that the lure of free money is no longer powerful enough to persuade millions of parents to surrender their authority over their children's education to the person holding the hammer.

I am calling for educational reform based on parents returning to the field of education, money in hand, and demanding the right to educate their children in the way they see fit. The cost of educating the children is not just the cost of buying materials, however. It is also the cost in forfeited time and forfeited money: the parents, or least one of the parents (usually the mother), must devote time to educating the children. If a parent must leave the workforce to do so, this expense must be borne by the family. These are real expenses, and must of course be taken seriously on a case-by-case basis.

Then there is the additional problem of the latchkey child. Both parents generally now work full time. So their children are left unattended in summertime and after school. To overcome this problem, parents have to spend money to enroll the children in educational programs or for a nanny to monitor them. So, the total cost of education is larger than is usually assumed.

The latchkey issue usually begins when the child is eleven or twelve years old. The parent is not allowed by society or by the state to let an elementary school child wander around without supervision, or even stay at home without supervision. It is assumed a child is at risk under these circumstances, and the parent must pay to offset that risk. So, all the money spent to offset the risk of the latchkey child should be deducted from the cost of homeschooling the child. If the parent has to pay hundreds of dollars a month for supervision for a young child, then this has to be deducted from the net income earned by the parent in the workforce. So, when the parent pulls out of the workforce in order to educate the children, the expenses of supervision of the latchkey child are avoided.

When you consider the cost of getting to work, buying a wardrobe, paying taxes on all earned income, paying for some kind of child care when the child is too young for school, putting up with the hassle of a boss, and paying to offset the costs of latchkey children, the net benefit of the lesser-income-earning parent remaining in the workforce may not be all that great after all. Parents should calculate very carefully what it costs for one of them to remain in the workforce on a full-time basis. If that parent could earn money at home by means of the Internet, as well as monitor her child's progress in education, it may turn out that it is cheaper to homeschool the child than to remain in the workforce. Of course, in many cases it is not financially possible for one of the parents to quit his or her job. But in many cases, it is.

Libertarians have a saying: "You don't get something for nothing." This applies to all aspects of education. The parents do not get free education from the public school system. Somebody has to pay for that system of education. When somebody else pays, parental authority over education declines. It may be worth it to some parents to suffer this decline, but parents who do not want to then have a responsibility to take steps to see to it that their children get the kind of education they think appropriate.

As more Web-based educational technology is released, the costs of private education will continue to decline, and increasing materials will be demanded. This is what has been taking place in the United States for a generation. *This is the economic foundation of a true revolution in education.* The details of the curriculum materials, or the approach to education, or other technical aspects of Web-based education are minimal compared to the dramatic fall in the cost of educating a child at home.

———◦•◦———

Parental responsibility extends to every aspect of the educational program. Parents have a moral responsibility to understand what is in the textbooks assigned to their children. Yet how many parents sit down and read carefully through textbooks from kindergarten through twelfth grade? Hardly any. It is easier to assume that everything is all right. Why should they assume this? The liberal establishment has controlled the book publishing industry for the public schools for well over a century. The fads of liberalism extend into the textbooks.

The classic example of this is the textbook that high school football coach John T. Scopes used in teaching biology as a substitute teacher in 1925 in Dayton, Tennessee. The book was called *A Civic Biology.* It was published in 1914. Here are some extracts from that textbook:

> The Races of Man—At the present time there exist upon the earth five races or varieties of man, each very different from the other in instincts, social customs, and, to an extent, in structure. These are the Ethiopian or negro type,

originating in Africa; the Malay or brown race, from the islands of the Pacific; the American Indian; the Mongolian or yellow race, including the natives of China, Japan, and the Eskimos; and finally, the highest type of all, the Caucasians, represented by the civilized white inhabitants of Europe and America...

Improvement of Man—If the stock of domesticated animals can be improved, it is not unfair to ask if the health and vigor of the future generations of men and women on the earth might not be improved by applying to them the laws of selection. This improvement of the future race has a number of factors in which we as individuals may play a part. These are personal hygiene, selection of healthy mates, and the betterment of the environment...

Eugenics—When people marry there are certain things that the individual as well as the race should demand. The most important of these is freedom from germ diseases which might be handed down to the offspring. Tuberculosis, syphilis, that dread disease which cripples and kills hundreds of thousands of innocent children, epilepsy, and feeble-mindedness are handicaps which it is not only unfair but criminal to hand down to posterity. The science of being well born is called *eugenics*...

Parasitism and its Cost to Society—Hundreds of families such as those described above exist today, spreading disease, immorality, and crime to all parts of this country. The cost to society of such families is very severe. Just as certain animals or plants become parasitic on other plants or animals, these families have become parasitic on society. They not only do harm to others by corrupting, stealing, or spreading disease, but they are actually protected and cared for by the state out of public money. Largely for them the poorhouse and the asylum exist. They take from society, but they give nothing in return. They are true parasites.

The Remedy—If such people were lower animals, we would probably kill them off to prevent them from spreading. Humanity will not allow this, but we do have the remedy of separating the sexes in asylums or other places and in various ways preventing intermarriage and the possibilities of perpetuating such a low and degenerate race. Remedies of this sort have been tried successfully in Europe and are now meeting with some success in this country.

Believe it or not, this was the standard liberal line in 1925. Two years later, this outlook was used by the Supreme Court to legalize the state-forced sterilization of supposedly retarded women. The case was *Buck v. Bell*. It has never been overturned by a subsequent Supreme Court decision.

Parents enroll their children in private schools. They hope that the textbooks will not be anything like *A Civic Biology*. But if parents are not willing to read the assignments, then they are forced to trust the headmaster of the private school in the selection of textbook and other course materials. The headmaster in turn has to trust the teachers. This is akin to a chain of command. The people at the top are not really sure what is going on at the bottom.

I am not saying that every parent has to read every textbook. Parents have to make decisions regarding whom they rely on to provide the textbook materials in classroom instruction. But homeschooling parents have a much better opportunity to investigate what is being taught than other parents do. They can read any of the curriculum materials for themselves. They see themselves as more responsible, so they are more apt to pay attention to what is being taught.

A homeschool parent has this advantage: if he does not like a particular textbook, he can substitute another textbook. He does not have this degree of authority even when he sends his child to a private school. He must accept the overall program of that school. This is not the case when parents teach their children at home. They have far greater authority to substitute materials when they are homeschooling parents than they do when they are parents of children in private schools.

To sum up, parents have a moral and legal responsibility to educate their children. This authority can be delegated, but parents do not escape the responsibility by delegating this responsibility. They remain the primary agents of education.

Parents decide which programs and materials are best for their children. Most parents do not give this much thought. But this does not in any way lessen their responsibility. They still decide. This decision is an inescapable concept. A decision not to adopt a particular program is a decision to adopt another program. The state's system of compulsory education forces this decision on every parent.

The availability of homeschooling materials, and of online education, makes possible far greater authority over education. There is a wide range of materials. The costs of buying online instruction keep falling. The old rule of economics is true: "At a lower price, more is demanded." This is why homeschooling is growing in popularity.

5

COMPETITION IN EDUCATION

I n college-level textbooks on economics, there is always a chapter on monopoly. The textbook goes into considerable detail on the nature of monopoly, and how it hurts customers. The heart of the chapter is the discussion of how suppliers use government to restrict supply, which enables the suppliers to charge higher prices for their output. Customers cannot go to rival suppliers in order to meet demand. So they are forced to deal with those sellers in the marketplace that have a competitive advantage granted to them by government privilege. The discussion centers on the artificial limitation of supply, and how this reduces the wealth of customers because it reduces their choices.

I have never seen a college-level textbook go into detail on how the government regulates educational institutions. The discussions do not point out that the regulatory system creates a monopoly, a cartel, at the university level. It restricts the supply of advanced education. The chapter also does not discuss how education at the kindergarten through twelfth-grade level is not merely a cartel but also a state-subsidized system. These subsidies keep out competing programs that are not entitled to the state's subsidies. Furthermore, the regulatory system restricts the supply of teachers, schools, and educational programs. By any standard, the educational system is either a monopoly or at least an oligopoly (consisting of a few sellers). The entire regulatory apparatus, when combined with the system of tax subsidies, has produced a system of education marked by artificial limits on supply and high prices.

In the case of tax-funded education, the high prices are concealed from the voters. It is not clear what the cost per child is in any given school district. It is also not clear what percentage of the total budget goes to administration, as contrasted with classroom teaching. Voters find it very difficult to sort out who gets what with respect to the money spent by the local school system. There is a decided lack of transparency. This is to the advantage of the bureaucrats who control the educational system, and it is especially advantageous to the administrators who benefit most from it.

———•·•———

The free-market doctrine is that there should be open entry into labor markets, capital markets, and the markets for goods and services. This open entry guarantees diversity. It provides a large number of choices to consumers. Consumers can match their desires with the available supplies of goods and services.

The potential for profit lures suppliers into the marketplace, and their presence ensures a wide variety of choices.

The free-market principle of open entry is challenged by governmental restrictions on access to consumer markets. There are many official justifications for these restrictions, but the main one is this: "Customers do not know what is good for them." They do not know what products to buy, what prices to pay, or what arrangements to negotiate with respect to return and replacement. Customers are in fact woefully ignorant of what they really need, so the state enters the marketplace to restrict what customers are legally allowed to purchase. The idea here is that state officials know what customers really need as distinguished from what customers are willing to pay for.

One of the justifications for this is that advertising deludes customers. This means that customers are considered not able to sort out fact from fiction when they read or see an advertisement. It is interesting that the same advertising agencies hired by businesses to sell products are also hired by politicians to produce advertisements in election years. In other words, advertising is accepted as a legitimate way to motivate people to take action during election years, but is placed under suspicion when it comes to advertising products and services. People in their capacity as voters are supposedly perfectly capable of making accurate decisions based on advertising. On the other hand, those same people in their capacity as customers supposedly are incapable of making accurate decisions based on advertising. This is utterly illogical, but it is basic to understanding all modern governments in the West.

The state creates restrictions on entry into certain fields. The government says that customers must be protected by regulatory agencies. Regulatory agencies screen out sellers of goods and services that have not met certain government criteria. The assumption here is that the regulatory agencies are capable of specifying product quality, and that in order to enforce these decisions, the government is authorized to impose negative sanctions, such as fines and even jail sentences. This assumes that bureaucratic standards of quality are superior to those of the marketplace. Customers are supposedly incapable of enforcing these standards in the marketplace. This is the reigning assumption of regulatory agencies everywhere.

Whenever the state intervenes in a market to restrict entry by sellers, it results in higher prices. Customers are not able to buy the kinds of goods and services they want, at a price they are willing to pay. So the producers who would otherwise have entered the market are forced to enter other markets. These markets are less profitable than the restricted markets. Customers in the regulated markets are worse off, and so are marginal suppliers who leave those markets.

———•———

We can see this principle at work in the market for education. The supply of education is limited by government restrictions on academic certification. Teachers must go through a specified regimen at the college level in order to be eligible to teach in the nation's tax-funded school systems. This reduces the supply of teachers who can legally be hired by local school districts. Furthermore, restrictions on school construction by private entrepreneurs limit the amount of competition tax-funded schools face.

So, parents are compelled to send their children to school, but the state restricts the number of schools available to parents. This creates a near monopoly of education, kindergarten through twelfth grade, for the state. The state uses tax funding to build schools, and it uses the regulatory system to restrict the creation of rival schools. This is the classic mark of a monopoly.

The free-market solution is open entry and competition. Competition may be in the form of quality. Some parents want very-high-quality education for their children, and are willing to pay a great deal of money to purchase it. They would not have to pay as much money if there were open entry into the local market for schools. Other parents cannot afford the best education for their children, because they do not have enough money. So, they want price-competitive education. This is also made available by entrepreneurs in the field of private education. These entrepreneurs can decide which programs are affordable for which parents, and which programs will meet the demands of specific parents. As more schools come onstream, the range of choice for parents increases. This is the standard definition of what constitutes economic growth. Economic growth takes place when customers can buy more goods and services than they were able to buy prior to the increase in economic growth.

As I said, the libertarian begins with this principle: "One size does not fit all." This applies to the field of education.

The solution is open entry into the field of education. Producers can specialize. They can target specific groups within the society. Entrepreneurs can provide education at a competitive price. The range of choices available to parents increases. There will be competing systems with respect to educational methodology. There will also be competing systems with respect to the content of education. Parents have a greater range of choice, but of course this means that they must spend more time researching the marketplace. They must find out what is available and at what price.

When parents have this degree of authority, they can exercise their responsibility at a much higher level. They can concentrate on what curriculum materials are available. When the supply of these materials is limited by law, this reduces the range of choice available to parents, and therefore reduces the degree of responsibility parents are capable of exercising. If something is not being made available, the parent is not responsible for the fact that he did not investigate it, evaluate it, or even purchase it.

———— · • · ————

Bureaucrats in the field of education, which is almost exclusively nonprofit education, have a bias against price-competitive academic programs. They assume that these programs are of low quality. They think it is a good idea to close the market to sellers of any kinds of curriculum not certified by educational bureaucrats. They have greater control over the content and structure of education when they can restrict entry into the marketplace. In the name of helping children, these promoters of self-interested restrictions on entry conceal the fact that they are able to exercise greater power over education and then charge more for the privilege of doing so.

This is why libertarians believe that there should be open entry into the field of education. They do not trust state bureaucrats to act on behalf of parents, especially parents who have a particular view of the best methodology and content for the education of their children. The bureaucrats operate in their own self-interest, which is to expand their power and income.

This raises the issue of government regulation of schools. First, the government requires compulsory attendance. Second, in order to keep control over the content of the curriculum, governments establish rules and regulations governing those schools. Parents are not allowed to send their children to schools that do not meet these qualifications. The qualifications are set very high, so that not many schools can be established to compete against the public school system. This increases the power of the public school system, and the power of the bureaucrats who run the system.

An example of this kind of regulation can be seen in the requirement that private high schools have libraries of at least 1,500 books. States around America had this requirement or something similar to it in the 1990s. But a student in the early 1990s was able to carry a CD-ROM with 5,000 books on it: the Library of the Future. No matter. A CD-ROM and computer stations did not count as meeting the 1,500-book requirement. The books had to be physical, so tax money had to go toward that. Today students have access to hundreds of thousands of books by means of the cell phones in their pockets. But accredited high schools must still have physical libraries. These libraries must be run by someone with a degree in library science. Conclusion: The library requirement has nothing to do with number of books in the library. It has everything to do with increasing the cost of building a facility that qualifies as a school that meets the government's regulations.

The goal of academic regulation is to limit the supply of schools that compete against public schools. This is done in the name of guaranteeing the educational quality of the school, thereby protecting the students. Yet the academic performance of the public schools continues to decline, and has done so since the early 1960s. The scores on the SAT and ACT exams continue to fall. The high point was in the early 1960s. So, regulation has not been successful in guaranteeing the quality of education. But it has been quite successful in restricting entry into the field of education.

In the 1980s there was a great battle over homeschooling. States around the nation passed laws prohibiting parents from substituting homeschooling for schooling in either a tax-funded school or a private school. The private schools were so expensive that only a handful of parents could afford them. This meant that parents would simply have to send their children to the public schools. The appearance of homeschooling in the 1970s and '80s represented a threat to this strategy of restricting the supply of competing educational programs. States prosecuted parents for teaching their children at home.

A major case was tried in Texas in 1985, *Leeper v. Arlington*, in which a coalition of homeschool advocates brought a class-action suit against the state. The state lost the case in the state supreme court in 1994. The court required school districts to compensate the parents of the children who brought the suit.[1] This case sent a clear message to local school districts in Texas. Overnight, they removed most of the restrictions against homeschooling. The state of Texas became very friendly toward homeschooling. But it took a court case to achieve this goal.

———•—•———

Parents should exercise their legal authority to establish whatever kind of curriculum and structured environment they deem appropriate for their children. This assertion of authority is deeply resented by the states' educational bureaucrats, who for more than 150 years have waged a war against parental authority in the field of education in the United States. The idea that parents have sufficient judgment to determine the education of their own children is rejected automatically within those institutions of academic certification that train public school teachers and administrators. The critics argue that some parents will not care enough about the education of their children to go to any trouble to provide a curriculum for them. They argue that the state has an

---

1. http://bit.ly/LeeperCase.

obligation to mandate the proper instruction of those children.

It should be obvious why this argument is not sufficient to establish a massive bureaucracy that regulates all educational programs. If the vast majority of parents did not care enough to educate their children well, they would have the power politically to elect representatives who would strike down all such laws. Rather, the only way that such laws get passed is because the majority of voters believe that the state does have legitimate authority in establishing compulsory attendance laws and regulations regarding the kind of curriculum assigned to students. This is a case in which educational bureaucrats blame a nonrepresentative group of parents, who in fact constitute a small percentage of the members of the community. On the basis of defending the children of these households, the bureaucrats persuade politicians to pass comprehensive compulsory education laws and other regulations governing private schools that meet the standards of the compulsory education laws.

Compulsory education laws and other regulations rest on the assumption that the state has a moral and legal obligation to supply benefits to specific groups of citizens. In this case, the citizens are not yet of voting age. This is an extension of the idea of the state as a healer. The state is supposed to intervene to make things better for certain groups inside the state's jurisdiction.

When we see these kinds of laws, we also see the expansion of state power into areas of our lives that ought to be left alone. If there are individuals in the community who are not providing a proper education for their children, the question then arises: Who has the legitimate authority to determine what constitutes a proper education for children? Also, what power should the state transfer to these people who claim they have the ability to determine what constitutes a proper education for children?

By establishing criteria of academic excellence, the bureaucrats have been granted the power to stifle educational innovation. There may be all kinds of programs and technologies available to educators that are not being used by the tax-funded school system. These technologies and innovations do not conform to the established criteria of the regulated school systems. They may rest on completely different theories of how children learn. They may use different technologies than those accepted and mandated by the tax-funded school system. They may constitute a true breakthrough in education. But schools are not allowed to adopt these technologies or approaches because these innovations do not meet the standards promulgated by state bureaucrats in the name of the legislature.

Government compulsory education and the associated regulations that define acceptable education restrict the freedom of parents to make judgments about the best educational programs for their children. Compulsory education and other regulations substitute a completely different hierarchical system over education. Bureaucrats make the rules, and force them on children under the jurisdiction of their parents. This assumes that bureaucrats, who seek to feather their own nests, possess wisdom regarding the education of children whom they have never seen. More than this, politicians assume that these bureaucrats have better insight into what is good for children in general than parents have for their particular children. This system assumes that the information available through bureaucratic chains of command is more relevant to the education of children than the information available to parents.

Why do we accept this as okay? Shouldn't the parents and local educators who actually *know* these children have the final say in this?

———

The libertarian position is simple: *parents have the authority to determine what kind of education is best for their children.* This means that the state should not interfere in the lives of parents and children with respect to the content and structure of their education. There should not be anything resembling a government monopoly of education. Standards that govern the public school system locally should not be imposed on parents who decide to remove their children from that system. *Without freedom of parental choice in education, the state will pursue a policy of extending its monopoly over education.* Tenured, state-funded bureaucrats will then use this monopoly to screen out ideas that call into question the legitimacy of government interference in many areas of life, including education. The government does not have to burn books in order to persuade the next generation of voters of ideas that favor the government. The government need only screen out books and materials that are hostile to the expansion of the state. The students do not gain access to such materials except at home, and the hours spent learning at home are minimal compared to the hours spent in tax-funded schools.

Parents who are convinced that the curriculum materials in the tax-funded schools are not what they want for their children should be allowed to provide alternative curricula in the privacy of their own homes. This is what educational freedom is all about. If parents want to pull their children out of the tax-funded school system, there should be no restraints on their doing so. There should be no restraints on the development of curriculum materials. The adoption of specific curriculum materials should be left to the parents' discretion. It should not be a matter of civil law.

6

SELF-INSTRUCTION

At some point in every student's academic career, he must move away from instruction by teachers and toward self-instruction. The obvious example of someone who has made this transition is a person who has passed his oral examinations for a doctorate degree and is now working on his dissertation. But the transition from classroom instruction to self-instruction takes place long before a student enters a doctoral program.

———•———

Classroom instruction is not efficient. This is why we find that, once a person graduates from high school, college, or graduate school, he never again subjects himself to anything like classroom instruction, except maybe for a brief seminar over a weekend. Classroom instruction is not suited for the presentation of detailed new information. The lecture method is a good way to impart the highlights of a difficult topic. The highlights may create interest in the topic; that is what a seminar is supposed to do. But the idea that the lecture is a good way to communicate basic information, most of which is supposed to be remembered, is ludicrous. We know this because at least 90 percent of everything in a lecture is forgotten in less than three weeks.[1] It is almost random as to what information in a lecture is actually retained by the listener. What one listener will retain will be very different from what some other listener will retain.

This is why classroom instruction is a poor substitute for reading. With reading, a person can skim over the information rapidly to get a sense of the overall perspective. Then he can go back and read at a slower pace. He may highlight certain information. He may make marginal notations. If he is wise, he records key facts and their location in a book by posting the information on Evernote, a "cloud" storage application. This way, he can come back and search for information a decade later, or half a century later. If he has made notes in the book, he can reread his notes, or skim the highlighted portions. He can review the material when he needs to. None of this is possible with a long-forgotten lecture. Even if the student recorded the lecture, it is not easy to review a lecture. The student can read at least twice as fast as, or maybe five times faster than, somebody speaks. He'd have

---

1. Tomorrow's Professor Mailing List, Issue 790, at http://tinyurl.com/
LectureLoss.

to listen to the entire lecture to find the piece of information he was searching for.

All this is to say that lectures are at best supplemental exercises in conveying new information. On the other hand, some people might be wired to learn better through a lecture than through reading. Other people gain mastery by careful reading. Still others are best taught through discussion. Again, as always, *one size does not fit all*.

When the student begins to make the transition from a classroom instruction environment to self-instruction, he begins to makes the transition to academic maturity. Academic training is supposed to be governed by this principle: *as a student becomes more mature, he becomes less dependent on any teacher*. He learns mostly on his own, and he approaches teachers for further illumination only when he gets stuck. Yet even here there is a compromise with teacher-based instruction. First, the student becomes dependent on a teacher to get him through the hard places. Second, he may not learn the techniques for mastering new and difficult information. Third, he becomes dependent upon a classroom environment. At some point, this comforting environment is going to be taken away. It is therefore best to wean a student away from classroom instruction as early as possible. This will be at different ages for different students. It may also be at different ages for the same student in different courses. But, at some point, the student has got to be kicked out of the nest. The classroom is the nest.

Because classroom-based education is geared to multiple students in a room, the principle of the lowest common denominator takes over. The teacher is tempted to concentrate on showing the least prepared, least intelligent, and least gifted student in the class how to master the material. The brighter students therefore get bored fast. They are being held back by the least competent student. In other words, classroom instruction favors the less-competent students.

If the goal of education is to maximize the learning experience of every student in the program, the best form of education is self-education. The student is not put into a classroom environment. He is not held back by slower students. If he is one of the slower students, he can review the material until such time as he is ready to go on to the next level. He does not become a liability to other people in a classroom. He does not feel as though he is the dummy. He does not feel singled out as the least competent person in the room. It is not good for a student psychologically to be at the bottom of the heap in a classroom. If he is at the bottom of the heap in several classrooms, he will be tempted to drop out of school. That kind of mind-set can persist into adulthood, when it may have been easily avoided.

This is a reason that homeschooling is superior to classroom education. The homeschool student can go at his own pace. If he is very good in a particular course, he moves ahead rapidly. If he has trouble with another course, he keeps reviewing the material until he is ready to go on to the next level. He sets the pace. He may set the pace in a classroom environment, but only when he is the one who learns slowly, and so becomes an object of derision. This is not the kind of mental attitude that favors personal progress in education.

Most students are ready to make the transition to self-taught education by the beginning of the sixth grade. Some students achieve this earlier. When the student is capable of reading without moving his lips, and of writing a brief summary of what he has read, he is ready to be placed in a self-instruction program. He has the fundamental skills to read and write. He can assess what he is reading, and express this clearly in writing. In a well-designed homeschool curriculum, the student begins writing no later than the fourth grade. Through the fourth and fifth grades, he develops his writing skills. By the sixth grade, he should be ready to learn on his own.

Such a suggestion horrifies professional educators. Professional educators have spent their lives thinking about how to make classroom education more efficient, or fairer, or less expensive, or whatever. An educator is focused on an environment in which learning rarely extends beyond graduate school, and probably should not go on much beyond the sixth grade.

What does a student need to become an efficient self-learner? He needs the ability to read rapidly. He can get by if he does not read rapidly, but he certainly has a tremendous advantage if he does. Second, he needs the ability to understand what he is reading. Third, he needs a way to help remember what he has read. Fourth, he needs to be able to express himself in writing. He needs to be able to put on a piece of paper or on a computer screen whatever it is that he has learned from his reading assignment. Fifth, he should also begin to develop the ability to verbally summarize what he has read, and even better, to integrate what he has read recently with what he has read over a longer period of time. In other words, he has to be able to think analytically, breaking down topics into their component parts, and he has to be able to think synthetically, which means putting the various parts back together into a coherent whole, one that he understands.

This kind of education is what sustains a person after he leaves formal education. This is what he needs to be a success in any field. This is what parents want for their teenage children. Yet the educational programs imposed on students by professional educators do not emphasize these important skills. This is because the lecture method in front of a classroom is slow, and is geared to the person in the room who is least academically competent.

It is all right to have a lecture. But it should not be aimed at the least competent student in the classroom. It should be aimed at whatever the target audience is. Maybe this is the student in the middle of the pack. Maybe this is the student who is the brightest in the class, except that there is no class. The lecture is posted online. It is digital. It can be easily viewed and reviewed.

———·•·———

One of the great mistakes parents make is to ask for small classrooms for their high school students. By the time a student reaches high school, he should not require any kind of intervention from an adult. He should possess the aptitude for self-education at this point. He should be able to master new material without continual intervention by any adult. It is best if he does this without any adult intervention at all. This may not be possible in all cases, but it should be possible in most cases.

The parent who demands that his child be given special attention by a high school teacher is making a big mistake. That student is being coddled. When he walks onto a college campus, he is going to be blindsided. There will be nobody there to look over his shoulder. There will be nobody there to encourage him. There will be nobody there to nag him. He will be almost entirely on his own. Nobody will tell him to go to class. Nobody will tell him to participate in course discussion groups.

The student who has received specialized attention all through high school finds himself completely on his own when he enters a college. He is not self-confident, because he has not been involved in a program of self-education. His only hope is that others in the classroom have been similarly coddled.

———•◦•———

If what I say is true, then why does the student have to go off to college at all? Why does he have to go into a classroom environment? Why does he have to listen to lectures, especially lectures delivered to hundreds of students in a large lecture hall? Why is he subjected again to an inefficient system of education? The answer is simple: It is traditional. It goes back almost a thousand years, to the very first medieval universities. There were no books for most students at that time. The printed book did not appear in the West until the mid-1400s. So students had to write down the material. They listened to a lecture; they wrote very fast. This mode of education stretched back to priestly classrooms in ancient Egypt. This is how education was always conducted. But when movable type became used in the West to produce books, this ancient form of education became far less efficient when compared to the educational system based on the careful reading of printed books. The continuing justification for classroom teaching was that this enabled students to interact with one another and with the professor. In other words, it was some form of Socratic dialogue. It was not based on the lecture system.

The fact that university students today are expected to sit at a desk and write down notes from a live lecture is silly. It is a denial of the power of the printed page and the video lecture. In the twenty-first century, it is also a denial of the power of digital communications. Why in the world are students required to sit silently at their desks, frantically writing down what they hear in a lecture, always falling behind, because they cannot write as fast as the professor is lecturing? It is preposterous, and it is universal. Parents are asked to pay up to a quarter million dollars to send the student to a major private university whose teaching methods became obsolete sometime around 1450.

This is not an argument against a tutorial system. A small class of students who discuss the material they have read is a legitimate form of instruction. It is the old Socratic method. But it is extremely expensive, and it is suitable only for students of the very highest caliber. It is used with undergraduates mainly at Oxford and Cambridge, as it has been for about a thousand years, and in graduate seminars everywhere.

———

Students need specially designed online courses that involve all three of the basic techniques of learning. First, there should be daily reading assignments. Second, there should be either daily or weekly writing assignments. Third, there should be introductory lectures geared to the reading assignments, in the form of screencasts. A screencast is an outline narrated by the person who has produced the outline. There may also be charts, formulas, or other tools for communicating numerical information. These lectures should be introductory, and they should be geared to help those students who learn better from a lecture than they do from an initial reading. A lecture should not be longer than about twenty-five minutes. Beyond twenty-five minutes, most students forget the material.[2] Only highly skilled lecturers can get away with longer presentations, and even then, the student is still going to forget 90 percent of it within about three weeks. A lecture should be geared to intro-

---

2. Donald Bligh, *What's the Use of Lectures?* 5th ed. (London: Intellect, 1998), chap. 5.

ducing students to new material, and then motivating them to pursue it. It should be a video.

If the student can master new material on his own, break it down into its component parts, and then put the parts back together in an essay, followed by a summary video lecture, he probably does not need to listen to a lecture in the form of a screencast. There is no reason for a student to subject himself to a form of education that gives him no particular advantage or the ability to learn new material faster. The student should adopt whatever approach to education works best for him.

If a student gets really stuck, it is legitimate for him to ask for help. But he would be wise not to ask the professor. He would be wise to ask a student who has successfully passed the course. The professor is still operating at a very high level, whereas a student who has passed the course is in a much better position to help another student master the material, because he remembers how *he* mastered the material. He did not have a mastery of the material when he started; he did have a mastery when he ended. He has sufficient mastery to be able to serve as a teacher. This is a better way to learn than to go to the teacher. The larger the number of students in a class, the less likely the teacher is going to be able to provide one-on-one assistance. Even a teaching assistant has limited time to take slow students by the hand and get them through the material. But if the educational program has forums in which students who have taken the class and done well can assist those not doing well, the program is more likely to produce a larger number of students who master the material.

Parents are afraid that their children will not survive in the competitive environment of college. This is a legitimate fear. But the way to deal with this fear is not to put the children in a high school classroom setting where the number of students is small and where the teacher can give individual attention to each student. *That is the worst way to prepare a student for the rigors of college competition.* The best way to prepare a student for that kind of competition is to put the student, no later than the sixth grade, into a self-taught curriculum program that separates him from a classroom teacher. This way, the student learns the techniques of self-instruction so that when he walks onto a college campus, he is not dependent on any professor or teaching assistant to get through the course. He is not dependent upon any third party to take him by the hand.

This is difficult for parents to accept. They do not think ahead far enough. They have forgotten what they experienced in college, or perhaps they did not go to college. They think that the training method of the classroom, preferably a small classroom, is the best preparation for the college environment. This places their children at a competitive disadvantage when they go off to college. The students have not learned the basics of self-instruction, self-motivation, and self-evaluation. They are still dependent on the lecture method. They are still dependent on their own note taking.

All this may seem new to you. If it does, that is because you are still locked into a mode of education that became technologically obsolete sometime around 1450. Traditions die hard. But eventually they die. And the tradition of classroom education is going to die soon enough, because the digital revolution is transforming collegiate education. This transformation is going to work its way down into high school programs. It is beginning, but it is not yet widespread. The teachers do not know how to use the new technologies. They are part of a bureaucratic system of education, and that system does not reward innovation.

Libertarians and conservatives should get a head start on this technological transformation of education. The sooner we help our children make the transition to self-instruction, the better it will be for them.

———•◦•———

We need to produce more leaders. Leaders do not find it difficult to make decisions on their own. They do not need to return to a teacher on a regular basis to master new material. A leader is someone who is capable of self-instruction at an advanced level, able to make decisions rapidly and confidently, and willing to bear responsibility for the outcome of any decision. We need leaders, and we do not get leaders by subjecting them to classroom instruction.

7

ONLINE EDUCATION

The future of education is online education. It offers many advantages over classroom education, but the greatest advantage is cost. Online education can be delivered free of charge to millions of people. This has already begun. It has begun at the collegiate level, and it has begun in kindergarten through twelfth grade.

Let us consider collegiate education. Six of the best colleges and universities in the United States have combined to post their courses online for free: Harvard, MIT, Berkeley, Georgetown, Wellesley, and the University of Texas (https://www.edx.org). When schools in the top tier adopt a program of free online education, we can be sure that this is the future.

To compete against this group, another group of universities, almost as prestigious, has combined to offer a comparable program called Coursera (www.Coursera.org). At present, about six dozen universities are involved, but this number is growing rapidly.

When you have the finest universities in the United States, plus several prestigious universities outside the United States, joining together to provide comprehensive classes in virtually every area of academics, you know what is going to happen to classroom education. Poor, bright students around the world will be able get their education online, free of charge. They may not decide to get their degrees from these institutions, but they can get course work from faculty members of the most prestigious universities in the world. The next step will be for these universities to grant certificates of course completion. These will not be the equivalent of a degree, but in the developing world, they will be worth a lot of money. They will be door-openers. People will still go to the best universities in order to access the old-boy networks that provide lifetime contacts and an entrée to good jobs. But, if we are talking about education, if these schools begin to grant certificates of course completion, conventional universities will be in big trouble.

In effect, these top-tier universities have "baptized" online education. Any critic of online education in general now has no plausible case. Here is the answer: "Are you saying that Harvard and MIT are not providing first-rate education online? Are you saying that digital technology is inherently inferior for education than the classroom model?" *When these schools decided to go online, they provided legitimacy for online education.* They broke the barrier. From now on, online education is in the arena of higher education. From this point on, online education will become a serious competitor at the collegiate level.

What about online education from kindergarten through twelfth grade? The premier program here is the Khan Academy. It has thousands of free videos for use by students around the world. The developer of the site, Salman Khan, earned a bachelor's degree at MIT. He earned an MBA from the Harvard Business School. Sometime around 2005, he began tutoring his young cousins and other family members in mathematics. Then, to speed up the process, he began posting videos of his tutorials on YouTube. One of his tutees told him that his videos were better than he was in person. At that point, Khan decided to create a website where he could post these videos. He began with basic arithmetic: one plus one equals two. After eight hundred videos, a student will have gone through calculus. Khan added other courses. In early 2013, one could find this summary of the Khan Academy on Wikipedia:

> The Khan Academy is a non-profit educational website created in 2006 by educator Salman Khan, a graduate of MIT and Harvard Business School. The stated mission is to provide "a free world-class education for anyone anywhere."
>
> The website supplies a free online collection of more than 4,000 micro lectures via video tutorials stored on YouTube teaching mathematics, history, healthcare, medicine, finance, physics, chemistry, biology, astronomy, economics, cosmology, organic chemistry, Amer-

ican civics, art history, macroeconomics, microeconomics, and computer science. Khan Academy has delivered over 240 million lessons.[1]

Bill Gates and other rich men began donating to the academy. It is now the premier teaching site on the Web.

There is no question by now that classroom *education in the liberal arts is going to become second-rate education as digital technologies improve.* Over time, the best education anybody can receive in most college majors will be online education. The competition is already becoming fierce. The best schools are posting videos of their best professors so that anyone can take their courses. The quality of these courses will be evident to anybody comparing them with standard classroom lectures in standard colleges delivered by standard professors. *The best and the brightest professors will be online free of charge.* A college that refuses to post its faculty members' courses will be suspected of being embarrassed by the quality of its courses. This will put pressure on all colleges to post their courses online for free. Students and parents will be able to "test-drive" courses. A lot of colleges will fail the test.

We are already seeing high school districts adopting online education. This is not done primarily for educational pur-

---

1. https://en.wikipedia.org/wiki/Khan_Academy.

poses. It is done for financial purposes. It is much cheaper for a school district to post a series of videos online than to bring students into the classroom. Online education is becoming popular in rural school districts where students must take buses for ninety minutes or more each way. A simple Google search of "online learning in rural school districts" will reveal numerous articles and resources on the subject. By consolidating school districts in the 1970s and '80s, these new geographically huge districts became economically liable for transporting students free of charge from their communities to central high schools: long drives, few students. Districts are able to cut these expenses by adopting online videos as the means of teaching students in their own communities, or even in their own homes. *The moment a school district does this, it is admitting that online instruction is as good as classroom instruction.* Any attempt by classroom teachers to say that this is third-rate instruction will meet resistance by the school district's administrators. If word gets out that the school is delivering a third-rate education, it will call into question the judgment of the school district. The administrators do not dare admit that any form of education they offer is third-rate education. Therefore, by posting videos online, and by moving students to distance learning, school districts legitimize these new technologies as being equal to classroom instruction.

The cost reduction offered by online education is so great that school districts around the United States will be tempted to add more and more courses to their online programs. *This is a major threat to the teachers' union.* An effective lecturer can be hired to teach a particular course to every student on a high school campus. The other teachers on the payroll who would normally teach the same course will be relegated to support status. School districts will be able to hire low-cost replacements of existing faculties, because these replacement teachers will do only low-level instruction: grade papers, make comments in the margins, and remain in the background. This means that all but the teachers most effective in front of a video camera will see their careers stymied. They will not get promoted. They will not get pay raises. They are easily replaceable. Legally, at present, a new teacher who is just out of college has the same certification as someone who has been in the classroom for twenty years but who is no longer needed.

Students can be taught by e-mail. If they have questions, they can e-mail one of the support-level teachers. The main teacher, who has all the exposure, and the highest salary, need not be bothered by students. This will be the prestige position on every high school campus. This is what the best and the brightest teachers will aspire to. There will be a new hierarchy of teachers. There will be the visible ones, who are effective in front of a video camera, and there will be all the rest, who are relegated to support status. This is an efficient way of dealing with education. It will enable school districts to cut costs.

There is an old rule in technology. When a new technology cuts the cost of operation by 90 percent, it always replaces an existing technology. The promoters of the old technology may complain, but it will do them no good. They can tell buyers that their old technology is worth the extra money, but the vast majority of buyers will not listen to them. When a new technology is ten times cheaper than an old technology, it is going to replace that old technology. The cost of delivering online education is no more than 10 percent of classroom education: no campus, no maintenance, no heating or cooling, no school buses, not much administration, no discipline problems, and software-graded exams.

Software-graded exams save money. This is how SAT and ACT exams are graded. So are CLEP exams. CLEP exams are produced by the College Board, which produces the SAT. CLEP stands for College Level Examination Program. Pass a CLEP with a score of 50 or higher, and you get full college credit. These exams are the basis for getting into a good college. The academic world honors these machine-graded exams. It is therefore possible, through online education, for one teacher to teach an unlimited number of students, with only a low-cost graduate university student grading essay exams and answering students' questions by e-mail. This is low-level work. It can be paid by the hour—no retirement plan, no healthcare insurance, no tenure. The main lecturer will get paid an above-average salary but will be able to teach every student on a high school campus the same course.

Let's go beyond this. Across the nation, successful teachers with advanced degrees will post their courses. A teacher can give away his lessons, just as Khan does. Or maybe he sells access at, say, $50 per year per student. He signs up, say, 5,000 students, or 10,000 students. School districts pay this tuition. Then they hire graduate students to grade the written exams, if any. You can see where this is headed. The students get the best teachers in the country. The local school district cuts the cost from, say, $11,000 per student to, say, $500. Maybe $1,000.

What is true of a high school teacher is also true of a college instructor. The University of Phoenix now has almost four hundred thousand enrolled students. It is the most profitable educational institution in the United States. It is fully accredited, and it is priced competitively. There are some schools that are far less expensive, but they are not well known. The University of Phoenix is significantly less expensive than most private colleges in the United States. That is because it has no campus. It has some rented space in commercial buildings. Go to this Web page: http://www.phoenix.edu/campus-locations.html.

If you click on it, up pops a Google map of locations near your zip code. There is no way that underfunded, campus-based schools will be able to compete with the extension of online education by universities that imitate the University of Phoenix. When you think that something in the range of twenty million students are enrolled in the United States, and one university has four hundred thousand of them, you get the picture. Most of the smaller schools are going to go out of business.

Online videos overcome many of the problems of classroom lectures. The main one is this: *you can back up a video and watch it again.* You cannot do this with a classroom lecture. The other advantages involve such things as visuals, links to other sites, and the use of that most remarkable of all encyclopedias, Wikipedia. You do not need a textbook if you provide links to articles on Wikipedia. Any teacher can compile a textbook from Wiki articles. They are in the public domain. He can add comments.

What is true at the college and public high school level is equally true of homeschool education. It is now possible to create an online homeschool curriculum that is offered free of charge. I have decided not to do this with my own curriculum, because I think that parents are willing to pay extra money to make certain their children have access to a unique curriculum with a certain viewpoint. I would use the tuition money for advertising capital. ("There ain't no such thing as a free advertising campaign.") The course designers are paid. Students will have access to forums in which they can interact with one another. By charging parents a fee, I eliminate students whose parents are really not very interested in the content of my education. I want students to deal with other students whose families are highly supportive of the worldview that governs my curriculum. There is an old phrase: "You get what you pay for." I think this is a good operating principle. But my goal has been to keep the cost low enough that any middle-class family can afford this program.

There will be a multiplication of online programs. This is a good thing. We need more competition in education. The greater the variety of educational programs, the better it is for families. Families will be able to select curricula that come close to the fundamental principles they are committed to. They will be able to supply their children with fully developed courses structured in terms of the first principles on which each of the families builds its future. For those families committed to the principle of limited government—federal, state, and local—my curriculum is the best thing available for them. Other families are not equally committed to this principle. They will have to seek out curricula structured in terms of whatever first principles they are committed to. That is what liberty is all about: choices.

There is no way that tax-funded education will be able to compete with the proliferation of free or low-cost curriculum programs. The main service that tax-funded schools will be able to provide is babysitting for eight months of the year. A few districts may be committed to rigorous academic programs, and will be able to generate revenue from outside their districts by charging tuition for online education to families outside the district. I expect that this will happen. A handful of public schools will become dominant in teaching students from around the nation. This competition is healthy.

There will be retired teachers who are effective in front of a video camera. They will be able to post comprehensive courses online. This means that they will be able to generate income based on their years of classroom instruction. There is no question that the number of such courses will proliferate when word gets out about the income potential for online education.

What about athletics? For parents who send their children to a high school campus so they can enjoy an organized athletics program or cheerleading or other activities, campus-based education will still be popular and will offer benefits. But for parents who are concerned most about the content, quality, and structure of their children's academic curriculum, online education is going to be increasingly popular.

There will be price competition. There will be ideological competition. There will be new technologies. There will be top-flight lectures. There will be alternative forms of certification, such as the CLEP exams, which enable a student to get college-level credit for work done in high school. All this benefits homeschool families.

What about shop classes? A school district can pay local businessmen to bring in students as unpaid apprentices. The student studies at home for half the day and works for half a day. This might cost $1,000 a year per student for a half day's work, which is cheap. It costs over $10,000 per student in most cities. The businessmen get paid twice: customers and the school district. Or a district can farm out this work to a charter school, which will train students. The district retrofits one high school for this purpose. It sells off the others.

With online education, the teacher can combine lecturing, an outline, readings in primary sources, links to videos, and links to classic materials in the public domain—and all of it can be delivered free of charge or at low cost. Students will not have to face the challenges that exist on every high school campus. The student will be able to go at his own pace. He will not have to interact with bullies and other negative aspects of compulsory education. He will not have to spend time on a school bus. He will not be tempted by sellers of illegal drugs or other peer pressure. He will be able to get up in the morning, pace himself in terms of his alertness, take a nap in the afternoon, and hold a part-time job during hours in which his peers are attending a campus-based high school. He will become far more competitive, and will be far more ready for a college experience, because of the fact that he did not set foot on a high school campus.

If he likes this kind of learning, he never has to set foot on a college campus, either. He can earn a bachelor's degree from an accredited college for $15,000 or less. He will not have to pay for room, board, or $150 textbooks. He can buy old textbooks on eBay or Amazon, and pay under $20. He can learn at his own pace. He can take examinations locally. He does not have to go off to college in order to get the benefits associated with an accredited college degree.

I want to tell you the story of Bradley Fish. He lives in Marietta, Georgia. He beat the collegiate system. He is the oldest of ten children, and his parents homeschooled him. At the age of fourteen, he decided on a plan of action. He would graduate from college on his eighteenth birthday. He went to work. He began taking CLEP exams and DSST exams, another way of earning college credits. He would study a homeschool course, study extra for the exams, and take them. One by one, he completed his college requirements. He paid for the lower-division exams out of his earnings from a lawn-mowing business. He borrowed some money for the upper division. For about $13,000, he completed his BA in business management the month he turned eighteen. The college that issued it is fully accredited. He repaid his loan from his parents within one year after his high school graduation, which was also his college graduation. He now makes a living showing students how to do what he did. He writes study guides on how to pass CLEP exams, and he manages a website where students can interact with one another as they prepare for the exams.

This is the wave of the future. The West's educational system did not adjust much to the invention of the book, but the Web is a far greater challenge to traditional means of classroom education than the printed book ever was. Online education provides most of the advantages that classroom-based education provides. The one exception is the science laboratory. Students can get most of their education online, at low prices, before they enroll in a campus-based program that offers them science laboratories. Not that many students major in science, however. In every other field, though, online education delivers an equal or better product than classroom education, and at a far lower price.

Classroom educators are going to have to adjust. This revolution of communications is not going to show any mercy to classroom teachers who are incapable of adjusting to these new technologies and implementing them in the lives of their students. When students finally learn that online education offers benefits equal to classroom education on a distant campus, there will be a shift to online education.

There is this risk: parents spend $50,000 to $200,000 on a campus-based education for their child, but the child fails to graduate. This happens in 50 percent of all cases. Then the student is at a disadvantage. He probably is in debt. The job market is tight. His years in college do not carry weight in the job market. At that point, the ex-student moves back in with the parents. These are called boomerang kids. Even if they had stayed in school all four years, they probably would have come home with $25,000 or more in personal debt. In some cases they come home with $100,000 in debt. With that amount of debt, they have then hurt their chances of getting married.[2] This is a terrible situation. But it is not necessary if the student and the parents know about the online alternatives.

———•—•—•———

By now, you understand why the revolution in education is imminent. The technology is now so inexpensive, and the cost of digital information delivery is essentially free of charge. It is now possible to produce highly creative educational materials with relatively little money. (It takes creativity, not money, to prepare a comprehensive, effective curriculum today.) Because it is possible to get high-quality materials online, there is no way a typical campus-based high school can compete. There may be one or two teachers on campus who are quite good, but most of them will not be, because most of the people in any organization are not that good.

Because of the Web, you can pick and choose among the best materials available. There will be more materials available over the next few years, and the quality will improve dramatically. Students are going to be able to be taught by the best

---

2. "Perfect 10? Never Mind That. Ask Her for Her Credit Score," *New York Times,* Dec. 25, 2012; see http://bit.ly/CreditScoreDating.

teachers in the world. This has never happened before, and it's going to change everything. It is going to take time, but it is going to happen.

———•◦•———

Here are some things to remember from part 2:

The educational reform I am proposing is revolutionary. It will transfer authority back to parents. This was unheard of as recently as 1960, except in certain religious subgroups. But the digital technologies that have appeared since 1990 have begun to drop the cost of educating students to levels undreamed of before 1990. This is the crucial factor: falling costs. This means falling prices. The old economic rule is taking hold in homeschooling: *when the price falls, more is demanded.* So, with respect to pricing, the revolution is already in a full-court press against traditional classroom-based education.

Public schools keep getting more expensive. Taxpayers are beginning to rebel. The cost of paying pensions and healthcare benefits to retired schoolteachers threatens every school district. As public schools get more expensive, homeschooling gets less expensive. There is no question where the United States is heading: away from tax-funded education and toward homeschooling. This is why my proposal is revolutionary institutionally but quite conventional economically. *The free market is going to foreclose on tax-funded schools.* There is no way that traditional education can survive the price pressure. As surely as paper-based newspapers are going under, so will campus-based education. This includes public school campuses. Forecasters who predicted the death of paper-based newspapers were correct. One by one, they are going under. The schools will be next.

Again, just look to the U.S. Postal Service. It cannot compete with FedEx, UPS, e-mail, and Facebook. It is a dinosaur. It is loaded with huge pension obligations. It cannot afford to make payments into this fund. This venerable monopoly has gone the way of all flesh. It recently announced that it may have to halt all mail delivery on Saturdays, but that is also only forestalling the inevitable. The USPS looked eternal in 1970. It looks like a candidate for a hospice today.

———•◦•———

This is the way to conduct a revolution: supply a better service or product. This takes no political revolution in the early phase. It takes only time. The free market can produce superior service to government non-enterprise. After a while, when most voters have stopped using the government's services, they can move on to the next stage of the revolution: refusing to pass any more bailouts. The voters tell the politicians to hold the line on all budget increases. They freeze spending. Then price inflation will cut costs.

This process of steady replacement is economically irreversible in education. Therefore, I am proposing a market-based systematic replacement for a state-funded bureaucratic system that will inevitably close its doors. The sooner parents have cost-effective alternatives available, the sooner they will decide to pull their children out of tax-funded schools. The sooner they pull out their children, the sooner there will be a tax revolt against the rising cost of public education. District by district, voters will elect politicians who will put a cap on spending. Then they will elect school board members who will vote to reduce the next year's school budget.

There will be fierce competition in education. One size does not fit all. I have no illusion that all the new online academies will teach a common curriculum. They won't. That is what freedom brings: diversity. We will get to see how committed to diversity some so-called open-minded people really are. We will see if some of them attempt to regulate the online programs in an attempt to force them to conform to a unified set of criteria proposed by the Department of Education in Washington.

The nation's most prestigious universities are going online. They are offering courses free of charge. They are declaring that online education is effective. How will local school districts resist the extension of online education? They won't. They will join the online revolution. They are already doing this in rural districts. But the day a district does this, it surrenders the argument that online education is inherently inferior to campus-based education. At that point, private-sector programs will gain acceptability.

Every reform must involve a change in funding. This change is now in progress. A family's out-of-pocket cost of educating a high school student online today is moving toward zero. The

Khan Academy has blazed the trail in zero-tuition education. Any high school curriculum that has a program of instruction that sells for under $1,000 a year, including books, can undermine a school district, which spends at least $10,000 and may spend $14,000 per student.

The local public school districts have accepted state and federal funding. They have therefore been forced to surrender control over local education. This was a bargain that removed the last traces of parental authority. But as the schools centralized, they alienated more parents. The principle of the lowest common denominator cannot be overcome by centralization. It is made even more unbreakable by centralization. Parents began pulling their children out of tax-funded schools.

As the price of online education falls, this exodus will accelerate. There is nothing like price competition to speed up institutional change. We have not yet begun to see the spread of low-cost educational alternatives. There will come a day in every school district when the exodus will become a flood. Call it a tipping point. Call it the straw that breaks the camel's back. It will come. The bureaucrats who run the public schools are as oblivious to this event as the bureaucrats who ran the Post Office were in 1970 (pre-FedEx) or 1995 (pre-Web).

———

This revolution is not merely about a shift in costs from high to low. It is also about a shift in benefits: positive for parents and students, negative for teachers and administrators.

The lecture method is traditional. It goes back to ancient Egypt. It could have been replaced by Gutenberg's printing press. But the tremendous hold on the literate elite that the lecture method enjoyed was not broken. Teachers have stood behind lecterns, lecturing to students who dutifully write as fast as they can. Unless students review their notes before the day is over, they begin to forget. Few students have ever reviewed their notes on the day they took them.

The online video/screencast is vastly more efficient than the traditional lecture. There is an outline, or charts, or items that cannot easily be communicated verbally. The student can watch it twice. He can pause it. He can back it up. If it is really good, it will still be teaching students in a year or a decade. It will survive. The lecturer will not.

The Internet will undermine the classroom lecture in ways the printed book did not. The book was expensive. The Web is essentially free. The book sometimes required a teacher to make it clear. The classroom was where students got help. The Web provides the teacher 24/7, anywhere a cell phone is. Who needs a campus? Who needs a lecture hall?

You may get only one lecturer per course on a college campus. In any case, you must juggle your schedule to get more. In high school, you are assigned a lecturer all year: no choice. But on the Web, you get as many lecturers as have commented on a topic, as long as a search engine can locate them.

At home, a student is self-paced. On campus, he is paced by the lowest common denominator.

In almost every area except activities, shop, laboratory work, and music, online education is better. These benefits will lead to an exodus from campuses. It is only a matter of time.

After the exodus accelerates, school bond issues will fail. Parents whose children are not on campus will vote no. Grandparents will also vote no.

The teachers' union will vote yes.

In part 3, I'll go into the bread-and-butter issues of my proposed educational revolution.

PART III
THE IDEAL SCHOOL

Whenever you consider the ideal anything, you should begin with this question: Ideal for whom?

Whenever you discuss the ideal anything with respect to economics, you must ask this question: Ideal from the point of view of the person who is paying?

Whenever you discuss the ideal anything from the perspective of a legal agent, you must begin with this question: On whose behalf does the legal agent act?

These are important questions. The main difficulty in discussing the ideal school is that multiple groups claim top position with respect to the decision-making process. Administrators in local public schools claim this for themselves. Teachers claim it for themselves inside the classroom. The school board claims it. If the school district takes money from the state, the state's Board of Education claims it. The Department of Education in Washington claims it. Courts claim it. Lawmakers at all levels claim it. Educational bureaucrats claim it.

The greatest advantage of homeschooling is that parents can claim it. They are the ones who pay for the program, assuming there is any payment involved. They are the ones who are acting as legal agents of their children. They interpret what their children need, and they select a program accordingly. Only to the extent that the state Board of Education has gotten the legislature to pass a law governing the content of homeschool curricula in general do the parents have to share this responsibility. These requirements are usually minimal, and most homeschooled children can easily meet them.

Ultimately, however, the student can veto the parents' decision. If a student decides that he does not like a program, he can complain endlessly, and at some point the parents get worn down. Or, if he chooses, the student can simply refuse to do any work. This is extremely rare, but it is certainly possible. Parents can impose negative sanctions, or promise positive sanctions, but ultimately the student can veto any curriculum.

The main reason I favor homeschooling, especially online homeschooling, is because parents have great authority in making decisions regarding the content and structure of the programs. They can reject all or a part of a particular curriculum. They are not trapped by all-or-nothing, take-it-or-leave-it offers. They can scrap one portion of a curriculum; they can substitute something else. They have far more authority over the content and structure of education when they are homeschooling their children online than they have with any other conceivable system of homeschooling, except one: where the parents create the entire curriculum on their own. This is so rare as not to be a factor in my consideration.

Because of the low cost of online education, it is now possible for parents to pick and choose among multiple curricula. But they have to do this as representative agents. They have their child's interest in mind. They want to pick a curriculum that will be good for the child in the long run, but that the child will also be sufficiently enthusiastic about to devote himself to mastery of the material. So, parents dare not ignore what their children want. The children do have some say in the matter, if only with respect to how much dedicated labor they will invest in the program.

Then there are considerations regarding colleges. If the child is on a college preparatory track, the parents have got to decide which colleges are acceptable and affordable. They also must decide if there are alternatives to conventional colleges. Should the children use CLEP exams in high school to reduce the cost of graduating from college? Are there other shortcuts that will save the parents tens of thousands of dollars? Parents these days tend not to ask these questions, because they are unaware that there are viable alternatives. When they are aware of the alternatives, they then find themselves in a negotiating position with the child. If they can persuade the child to take a lower-cost approach to college, they can adjust the high school curriculum accordingly. If the child agrees to this, families can save fortunes.

Then there is the question of the ideological or religious content of the curriculum. Are the parents satisfied with this content? Does the content correspond with the parents' first principles? Again, this is a matter of parental authority. The parents make these decisions amid a barrage of conflicting claims and issues. The parents have to get involved in a kind of juggling act to make good decisions on behalf of their children.

In putting together my online curriculum, I have considered all these competing claims. The old rule is true: one size does not fit all. I have attempted to put together a comprehensive curriculum that will meet the desires of the parents, the needs of the students, the admissions offices of colleges, and the available technologies of online homeschooling.

8

WHAT PARENTS WANT

Parents act as legal representatives for their children. This is a big responsibility. Each of the children in a family is different. Each child has different skills. Each has different interests.

If the parents do not choose private education, they are stuck with whatever the local public school is willing and able to provide. This means that the school system determines what the children will be allowed to experience. The parents have little input in the matter.

When parents are willing to pay for a private school or a privately marketed curriculum, they reestablish control over their children's education. They decide which academic program best suits each of their children.

In education, there are many kinds of students. There are many kinds of curriculum materials for these students.

One of the great problems with any system of tax-funded education is that the tax funding brings multiple levels of the state into the picture. In order for a school to qualify for tax funding, it must conform to certain requirements. These requirements move the entire educational system in the direction of bureaucratic management. In other words, government's money moves the educational system in the direction of "one size fits all." This is inherent in the nature of the funding. A state government cannot hand out hundreds of millions of dollars for education unless there are guidelines for spending that money. Otherwise, there would be a siphoning off of government funds to line the pockets of people inside the system. So, there have to be rules and regulations, and as a result, the entire system becomes bureaucratic. Ludwig von Mises called this bureaucratic management. He contrasted it with profit management.[1]

Bureaucratic management is always marked by a central source of money. The money comes from the state, and therefore it is controlled by state officials. Parents have only minimal inputs as to which tunes should be played, on which musical instruments, and in how large an orchestra. The educational system favors bureaucrats who have come up the chain of command inside the educational system. Bureaucracies are rarely innovative. The longer a bureaucrat has been on a payroll, the less innovative he is. The book of rules becomes

---

1. Ludwig von Mises, *Bureaucracy* (New Haven, CT: Yale University Press, 1944); see http://bit.ly/MisesBUR.

dominant: "We don't do things that way here." Bureaucracies are supposed to be predictable, but what is most accurately predicted is this: *a reduction in the influence of taxpayers over the system.*

Bureaucrats always resent interference from outside agencies, especially the legislature. So legislators can do very little to implement changes that are recommended by the parents of children enrolled in the local school system. Parents can do very little to educate the legislatures. So the top of the educational system is sealed off by the bureaucrats in terms of whatever this elite guild of educators favors.

The important principle to uphold here is that the parents should remain *economically* and also *legally* in control. The fact that they are willing to go into the private education market in search of a program that offers their children the best possible match indicates that they are willing to assert both their legal authority and their economic authority in the marketplace. They put their money where their mouths are. Their willingness to spend money and time on their children's education is the basis of their control over both the content and structure of education.

———•◦•———

What are some of the things that are most important to parents who take their children's education seriously? First, they want to make certain their children are safe. They want to make certain they are not subjected to bullying by other students.

In addition to safety, parents want a solid moral environment for their children. These days, the public schools have become the equivalent of drug emporiums. A lot of students are concentrated in one area, and they become easy marks for other students who are making money by selling drugs to their peers. Parents who are concerned about this can deal with it by removing their children from the environment. Children who are academically successful and self-confident about their abilities are less likely to succumb to the lure of fantasy escape provided by drugs.

Parents also want to make certain that teachers are concerned about their children's special educational needs. The trouble is, in a classroom environment, teachers have a lot of students to consider. They are restricted in the attention they can give to any one student. The student has to adjust to the teacher's abilities rather than the other way around.

As the student grows older, he is supposed to become more independent. This is important, because as I have said, when the student sets foot on a college campus, there will not be anybody there to act as his nanny. So, the high school curriculum, and the structure of the educational program, must be focused on the student's ability to mature. The student must become increasingly self-educated. *The entire academic program should be structured in terms of this process of maturity through self-education.* Parents tend to neglect this aspect of education, especially in the high school years. They want for their children in high school what they wanted for their children in the primary grades. They want individual attention for them. This is a mistake.

A student who begins as a freshman in college may be required to take classes that consist of as many as five hundred or even a thousand people in an auditorium. A professor lectures to the students. The students take notes. Then, several times a week, they meet in discussion groups led by graduate students who have no training in teaching. These courses are sometimes called mega courses. They are highly profitable to colleges. The cost per student is low: one professor and some low-paid graduate school teaching assistants. There is almost no individual attention associated with these classes. Students who are not self-disciplined, and who do not have good study habits, rarely make it through the first two years of college. This is why the graduation rate is only about 50 percent for students who enter as freshmen.

Parents should examine the high school curriculum very carefully to make certain that both the structure and content of the course work push the student, yet also provide a way for students to interact with one another. Students generally respond better when they are part of a program in which there is mutual interaction. A system of tutoring is exceptionally effective, because students understand what other students are going through. A student who has successfully completed the particular course has the experience of taking that course fresh in his memory. So, he is in a position to give guidance to the student who is just beginning the course. The teacher has not taken a course like this in a decade or more. The teacher forgets what is like to be a student. This is one of the great advantages of online education. Students can use forums to help one another over the rough spots, course by course. Another huge advantage is this: a student learns more as a teacher than he does as a student. *The experience of teaching somebody else is one of the best possible ways to master course material.* To use an analogy, teaching etches the material into the mind of the teacher. It is an extremely effective way to become proficient in a field that is new to you.

Parents are also concerned that the content of the curriculum is consistent with their first principles. They do not want teachers with a rival worldview to gain control over their children for six or seven hours a day. They do not want people with a rival worldview to sit in judgment of their children, pressuring them to abandon their parents' worldview and substitute the teachers' worldview. This process begins very early, but certainly it begins at the junior high level and continues all the way through graduate school. For centuries, teachers have seen their responsibility as persuading students to abandon the traditional views of their parents. This is why parents must be conscious of this conflict. Schooling is a recruiting process. Parents who are unaware of this are sitting ducks.

Parents who understand the nature of this confrontation can reduce the risk of seeing their children picked off by teachers. They do this either by hiring teachers as tutors, or by enrolling their children in private school classroom settings in which the teachers are more likely to share their worldview. But both these approaches are very expensive. Most parents cannot afford either option. This is the tremendous advantage the Internet offers to parents today. There are comprehensive curriculum programs on the Web that cater to the outlooks of a wide variety of parents. If the parent can find an online curriculum, or an online school that uses a particular curriculum, they can turn their children over to these online institutions. They can monitor what is taught in the classroom, because the classroom is located inside their own homes.

This is a crucial advantage to online education. Unlike all classroom education, *parents can monitor what is being taught their children*. They can look at the reading assignments. They can look at the examination questions. If there are videos involved, they can watch the videos, or at least sample the content of whatever is being taught. If a particular course is not to their liking, they can substitute a completely different course by going to a different website. Parents in effect can hire digital tutors.

Another advantage of online education is that parents can monitor certain courses and then discuss those courses with their children. One parent may monitor a history course. Another may monitor an economics course. After dinner, they can sit at the table and discuss what the child learned that day. The parent can also monitor the homeschooled child's performance by having the child pass a CLEP exam after every course. This provides evidence that the student has completed the requirements for a college-level course. There is nothing more persuasive to a truant officer than a stack of CLEP exams in which the student has scored at least 50 points (the cutoff score for acceptance in a college program).

Even if the student does not take CLEP exams, the parent can see that the student is performing well when the student writes a paper every week for each of his liberal arts courses.

The parent can see the improvement in the student's performance as he matriculates to the next year's courses.

Another advantage of online education is that the parent can assess the value of the program in a direct fashion. With tax-funded schools, parents really do not know what courses cost. Furthermore, they do not know about the allocation of funds. Is most of the funding going to the school's administration? How much is going to classroom instruction? This is almost impossible to discover, because the administrators make it very difficult for the Board of Education to discover the answers, and the Board is not interested in promoting widespread understanding of fund allocation among voters. This is especially true in districts where the lion's share of the money goes to administration.

When a family adopts homeschooling, the parents can easily assess how much each course costs. Is the course worth it? Most online schools offer a thirty-day money-back guarantee. If the parent finds that the particular course is not appropriate for his child, he can inform the administrator of the online curriculum that he wants his money back. This is not economically possible with any other form of education.

Because there are no government subsidies for online education, the federal government has no say over the content or structure of the educational program. There may be state regulations that force homeschooling parents to conform to certain course requirements, but in most cases, the child demonstrates through an examination that he has mastery of a given field. There is no question that an online course is an effective way to teach children. Most children involved in homeschool programs test higher than children of the same age in public schools.

If the parents really believe that a child needs a lot of adult supervision, one of the parents can specialize in a particular course. That parent can work with the child to get him over any intellectual barriers the course has created. I generally think this is not a good idea, for the reasons I have already mentioned. But if the parent disagrees with my assessment, he is in a position to intervene. If he thinks the child is not getting special attention, the parent can provide that attention. Obviously, this is probably not going to be the case in advanced calculus, but it can be the case in history, government, and maybe economics.

The parents can see which courses pose bigger problems for a particular child. This is important. The parent discovers through a system of examinations and writing assignments whether the child is progressing. The parent can see where the roadblocks are. While I think it is best to let the student find ways to get through or around these roadblocks himself, parents who disagree are in a position to intervene. The parent is in control. The parent delegates certain aspects of the course work to the designer of the curriculum, but the parent can always veto the creator of the course. If the parent thinks he has a better approach to teaching his child, he can intervene.

With online education, parents have a far greater choice of curriculum materials and structured education than is true with any other form of education. The parent does not have to pick a particular curriculum, or a particular course. He may decide to, but he does not have to. It is not an all-or-nothing deal. When he enrolls the child in a private school, it is very close to an all-or-nothing deal. There are probably not a lot of competing private high schools locally. But online, there are innumerable courses available.

———•———

The best curriculum is an integrated one. It is a curriculum in which the courses reinforce one another. Think of a course in history. It presents an era or a society as a unit. Although it is a separate area of study, the literature course should parallel that history course so the student can understand the society's literature as part of an integrated whole. So the literature course should reinforce the history course. The history course becomes more memorable because the student is familiar with representative examples of each society or era.

Think of American history. The course in civics should be tied to it. There should be a separate course on the Constitution and its development. There should be representative examples of American literature. These should be taught as representative examples of historical trends, not simply as stand-alone documents for literary criticism. The student should understand why a given book or short story was important in the era in which it was published. American literature should help illustrate the story of America's history.

If you find a curriculum designed by somebody who shares your worldview, and if that curriculum is self-reinforcing, then this is an ideal approach to homeschooling. This is what I provide in the curriculum I have begun putting together. The history courses interact with the literature courses. In American history, there is a parallel course in constitutionalism. There are also courses in economics that interact with the main courses in history and government. All of it together comprises what some people call a package deal.

———·•·———

If, as you have read what a well-designed curriculum should be, you thought, "I wish I had taken a curriculum like that," you can still do it. There is nothing that says that this curriculum is limited to teenagers. Maybe you don't have teenagers in your household any longer. But there still may be a student: you.

Parents can get the education that was denied to them when they were teenagers. Maybe they went through the public school system, and the textbooks used in that school were hostile to what they believed. They can now take a course along with their children and get introduced to a different interpretation of the materials.

While parents may not be able to spare the time to watch videos, they can download videos into audio files, and play them during the day. These become ideal drive-time podcasts. If the videos are structured on the assumption that the audience may choose to listen to them, rather than watch them on a computer screen, they become materials that parents can adopt for themselves.

Obviously, this is not going to be possible in a course on mathematics. There, you need to be in front of a screen, and you need to watch the teacher's numerical manipulations on the screen. I am speaking here of economics, history, government, literature, and the liberal arts in general. It would also apply to courses on starting a small business.

If you are interested in finding out more about my curriculum, send an e-mail:

paulcurriculum@aweber.com

9

WHAT STUDENTS NEED

The key issue is this: which students? A second important issue is this: at which stage in their academic careers? The student in the first grade does not want the same kind of education as a student who is a junior in high school and preparing for college. The student preparing for college does not want the same kind of education as a student who expects to go into the trades immediately after graduation, or who plans to start a little home business.

This is why anyone who runs a school must be clear before he starts regarding which students he wants to serve. Some students want to go into the liberal arts. Others want to go into the sciences. Some students want to start a business after graduation. Some are interested in the fine arts. How can one school, or one curriculum, satisfy all these desires? Furthermore, whoever runs the school must keep parents happy, if it is a profit-seeking school. It is not enough to keep students happy. This is why one size does not fit all.

I am convinced that students are probably ready by the age

of fifteen to make the decision about what best suits their needs in terms of an academic program. Some students will be mature enough to make this decision; others will not be. Children have to persuade their parents regarding what they think is best for them. At some point, parents will have to defer to their children. This usually begins no later than the junior year of college. But, in deciding which college to go to, students have considerable input.

There are certain aspects of every school that the vast majority of students prefer. One of them is safety. What do students want to be safe from? The obvious answer is bullies. Bullying is a common feature in tax-funded schools. We have heard the tragic stories of students driven to suicide by bullying. Public schools have repeatedly proven themselves unable to deal with this problem effectively. This has led some parents to remove their children from the local public school, despite the expense.

Students also do not want to be subjected to what is sometimes called busywork. Busywork wastes students' time. It accomplishes very little, except to fill the day. Students resent it, and they have good reason.[1] They have to spend seven

---

1. In the 1984 movie *Teachers*, there is a character called Ditto. He is a teacher who forces students to copy Ditto-machine-printed material by hand. This work fills every class period. He reads the newspaper all day at his desk. One day, he dies while reading. No student notices that he is dead for several class periods.

hours per day or longer in school, and when they have little to show for it except having spent a lot of time on useless activities, they feel they have been cheated. They are correct.

The older a student is, the better his judgment regarding what he ought to be studying. We understand this when the child begins his sophomore year in college. He must select a major. He has to meet the major's prerequisites. In the junior year, he must begin his major. This is usually at age nineteen. Parents may not believe that a child of fifteen is capable of making such a decision, but brighter, self-disciplined students are in a position to make it. The student needs to consult with his parents. He may take an aptitude test. But, ultimately, the student ought to be able to make this decision, as long as he fulfills basic requirements for education that will enable him to advance to the next level of schooling.

Here are some of the basic features of every school program that benefits students who have advanced to the level of self-discipline required for success in education. I am not in a position to assess what is needed by students who are not self-disciplined, and who are C-average students at best. I am talking about students who want to go to college, or who want to start a business immediately after graduation from high school. These are students who have some idea of what they want to do after high school graduation.

A student wants to be confident that, assuming he performs adequately in terms of the school's curriculum, he will be able to advance to the next stage of education. If he wants to go to college, he wants a high school program that will get him into college if he gets a B average or better. He wants to know that he is not wasting his time in the program. Most high schools offer programs that enable students to achieve this goal.

———•—•—•———

Inevitably, education is a form of competition. This is why most programs issue grades. If they don't have grades, then they have milestones: matriculation. A student wants to know that he will be competitive with his peers after graduation, that he will not find himself playing catch-up. He will not want to walk onto a college campus ill-prepared. Therefore, a student knows that he needs academic skills that will let him compete successfully in college. Here are a few of the skills that every high school program should impart to its students.

1. Reading

The student needs to learn how to read effectively. This means he must learn to read fast. Most of us are slow readers. We did not learn the skill of speed-reading and rapid comprehension when we were in school. We are burdened with this throughout most of our lives. It takes a systematic program of speed-reading, begun at an early age, to enable a student to overcome the bad habits associated with reading. This is why my curriculum focuses every day on exercises that will help a student read much faster than normal.

Then there is the other burden of reading: the requirement that we understand what we read. This is usually achieved by techniques that are the very opposite of speed reading. We have to learn when to read rapidly and when to slow down, think carefully about what we are reading, and even write outlines in order to increase our knowledge. We cannot possibly apply techniques of careful analytical reasoning to everything we read. We have to understand the difference between material that can be read rapidly, and stored effectively in electronic format, and detailed written material requiring specialized techniques of analysis.

2. Writing

It is not good enough to be an efficient reader. If all we do is pour knowledge into our heads, and we do not learn how to organize what we have learned in order to get it down on paper or on a screen, then we have wasted our time. Maybe we have not wasted all our time, but we have wasted a great deal of it. So, basic to any curriculum, beginning no later than the fifth grade, should be weekly writing assignments. Every week, a student is required to produce an essay. It need not be a long, detailed essay, but it should be the equivalent of an essay that can be posted on a website. It should not embarrass the writer.

Every student should be required to set up a blog. Of course, a lot of students already have blogs by the time they reach high school. But every student should have a blog and post his weekly writing assignments on that blog. This lets other people see what he has written. Over time, the quality of the writing will improve.

Parents should read the essays, but they need not do detailed grading of the assignments. If the student writes on a consistent basis, week after week, year after year, he will improve his writing ability extensively. By the time he reaches college age, his basic writing skill will be intuitive. He will not have to go through the normal learning process that colleges used to require, and all of them still should require, to produce students who can express themselves in print.

3. Public Speaking

In addition to writing, a student should learn how to speak in public. This is an extension of his ability to write. In high school, there are not many opportunities for a student to learn how to speak, unless he takes a course in public speaking. Very few students do this. Schools should require students to produce regular verbal exercises. Not only does this dramatically increase a student's ability to remember materials, but it also teaches him how to summarize material accurately and persuasively. By the time a student graduates, he should have a basic understanding of how to communicate verbally in public. He will be way ahead of his peers, who get very few opportunities to do any kind of public speaking in their high school years.

4. Digital Media

If a student can write and speak, he ought to be able to translate these skills into publicly available formats: media development. The technologies keep changing. There is no way anyone can be sure a particular communications medium is going to survive over the next ten years, let alone the next one hundred. But we do know that two of them have extensive advantages. The first is YouTube; the second is WordPress. These two outlets are widely used and have extensive user support.

The ability to produce effective short videos to be posted on YouTube is an important skill for business. Most businesses do not have decent websites. If a student can master the basics of the technology of producing an effective YouTube video, and also learns the basics of advertising copywriting, he will always be able to earn a living. Students should be taught how to do this by the time they graduate from my program.

5. Academic Research

A student has to learn the basics of academic research. These techniques can be translated into a business environment. Students have to learn how to learn. The Web has made it possible as never before for students to do extensive research. They have to learn how to cut corners. They have to speed up the process. Business requires rapid production, and students ought to learn in high school how to do effective research in a brief period of time.

They also have to learn the kinds of research techniques that are important in college. While it is true that modern colleges do not require the same number of research papers they did half a century ago, enough colleges do require research papers so that students had better be trained before they go to college to write such papers. These techniques used to be taught to advanced students in high schools, but because they involve a great deal of time on the part of teachers, there has been a tendency in high schools in recent decades to deemphasize term papers. This is a major mistake. It cheats the students.

6. Time Management

To accomplish all this, students need to know the basics of time management. These techniques are not taught in college, except as electives for no credit, and they are rarely taught in high school. The sooner a student learns how to manage his time, the sooner he is going to advance his academic performance. People who go into the professions or into business have to become experts at managing their time. They usually learn this on their own...late. They may even read some books in time management. But the problem with this is they are forced to learn this skill on the job. It would be far better if students learned these techniques in high school, mastered them in college, and were ready to go into the business world or the professions without missing a beat with respect to their ability to maximize the efficiency of their time.

7. Goal-Setting

Time management is important, but even more important is goal-setting. This is not taught in elementary school, high school, or college. Goal-setting is one of the most important single techniques that anyone can master, and the earlier he masters it, the better it will be for him. No student should enter college who has not already developed the skill of goal-setting.

I believe that students are capable of beginning to set goals for their entire lives by the time they are twelve or thirteen years old. Not all students can do this, but some students can, and the ones who do this gain a major advantage over their peers. If a student sets lifetime goals by the time he begins his sophomore year in high school, he is going to maximize the time he spends in formal education until he finally graduates. Goal-setting lets the individual make effective use of his time, which then is made more efficient by techniques of time management. But just mastering techniques of time management is insufficient. A student has to know early in his career what he wants to do with all his saved time. Students are not taught this, by either parents or teachers, so they are hampered in their careers until such a time when somebody finally sits down and helps them learn how to set lifetime goals.

8. Job vs. Calling

As important as goal-setting is, there is something even more important: being able to distinguish between an occupation and a lifelong calling. Remember, the calling is *the most important thing someone can do for which he would be most difficult to replace*. If a student learns the difference between the job and the calling before he begins his advanced high school work, he can begin to assess the importance of both time management and goal-setting. The student must understand that, in most cases, he must be proficient in two areas. He must be proficient in whatever he does to put food on the table, meaning his job. But he must also be proficient in his calling. This is where he makes his legacy. This is where he achieves significance in his life, but it probably is not tied to high monetary compensation. It may be, but it probably will not be. A student who learns early in his career the difference between a job and a calling has a tremendous advantage over his peers, because this makes him more effective at setting his goals, and it also enables him to make better use of his time.

9. Study Habits

Students are not taught early enough the basics of effective study habits. They develop poor habits, and then it becomes very difficult for them to shake those habits. When they use ineffective or inefficient study practices, those practices become almost instinctive for them. Then, when they finally get to college, or even out of college, those bad habits are etched in cement. This is why it is crucial that students be trained in the techniques of effective study at the beginning of their high school career. Actually, it is probably better to get this kind of training no later than the seventh grade, but not many online programs provide these techniques. The student at the high school freshman level should be introduced to the basics of effective study. These basics involve time management, but also certain techniques not taught in high school and used effectively only in a homeschool environment.

10. Mathematics

In today's world, mathematics is becoming ever more important. The use of statistical techniques in the social sciences and history has increased dramatically over the last forty years. Students who do not do well in mathematics are penalized. Yet mathematics instruction at the high school level is usually haphazard. There will be only a few teachers who are very good, and who can motivate students to do much better in math than most of us did when we were in high school, but what we need is a systematic program of mathematics development. We have an example of this already online: the Khan Academy. It is free of charge. Any homeschooler can use these lessons to improve his ability in mathematics. Not to use them seems silly. Some public schools are beginning to use this website to help their students improve in mathematics.

11. Self-Pacing

Students should go at their own pace. In some courses, they are very skilled; they race ahead. No classroom of slower students should hold them back. In other courses, they take longer. They should be able to review lessons. If it takes three viewings of a video, or three readings of a document, so what? They should keep reviewing until they master the material.

Students must learn very early to be competitive. This comes a long time before high school. The problem with public schools in recent years is that they emphasize self-esteem, but not self-esteem based on performance. Theories of self-esteem that are not based on objective performance in a competitive environment are self-defeating. The student begins to think he is competent when in fact he is barely functional, and may actually be incompetent. We hear these horror stories all the time. A student graduates as valedictorian of his high school class, but when he gets to college, he flunks out. He did not have the skills he was led to believe he possessed. So, it is important for any school environment to offer opportunities for students to master the material in a competitive environment. This does not necessarily mean the student has to be given grades. What it does mean is that he is able to compare his output with the output of his fellow students. This is another reason, with my curriculum, we require students to produce YouTube videos and start a WordPress account. Students can then see how they are doing in comparison with other students in the same program. They can also learn from the skilled performers, whether the skills involve technical knowledge or simply personal abilities that have been improved by years of self-expression.

12. Tutorials

I believe in good teaching, but I believe that teaching should be in the form of tutorials. I think the best people to teach students are other students. Students who serve as tutors to other students improve their own skills of communication. They become far more proficient in whatever subject they are teaching. At the same time, other students can get the information they need from students who may be only a year ahead of them. The students who are being taught are being taught by people for whom the learning experience is still fresh in their minds. There is also the problem that the world has only a limited supply of really good teachers. This is why the use of course-specific teaching forums is important. One student may not be able to communicate the information in such a way that the struggling student is helped very much. But if two or three students answer the same question, and provide an effective teaching video to demonstrate a solution to the student's problem, the struggling student is more likely to understand.

I think it is best that students learn on their own. Self-teaching is the best way to learn anything. But there are times when we hit brick walls. At that point, it is better to be taught by someone who has previously hit that same brick wall, and who remembers how he got over it, around it, through it, or under it. It is best to be taught by someone who remembers how he went about solving the problem. This is why my curriculum relies heavily on student interaction as a means of providing specialized tutorials for students who hit brick walls.

———•◦•———

Any curriculum that does not provide all these benefits is a substandard one. Students in a traditional tax-funded school may pick up bits and pieces of what I have described here, but not all these techniques are provided in a systematic fashion. I think any student who reads this list is capable of understanding the benefits involved. Once the student understands the benefits, he is far more likely to pursue this course of study with more real enthusiasm than he would if placed in an environment in which these techniques were not taught on a systematic basis.

———•◦•———

I have covered this before, but it is so vital that I have decided to repeat the message. Some students would like a lot of individual attention. This makes them dependent on their teachers. Other students want to gain mastery on their own. I think the latter is the correct approach. I do not think it is a good idea for students to become excessively dependent on salaried teachers, meaning live teachers in a classroom. *The older the student is, the less he should become dependent upon teachers in a classroom.* Perhaps for certain kinds of scientific studies, in which laboratory assignments are crucial, he needs the presence of a technician. A course like this can be taken in a summer school program at a community college or immediately after high school graduation. The point is, the more the high school educational program is self-taught, the sooner the student learns the basics of academic success in upper-division work in college. The closer someone gets to the final stage of the PhD program, the less dependent he is on any teacher's intervention. The brighter a student is, and the more self-disciplined, the less he should be dependent upon classroom teachers. If he needs help, he ought to get it from other students who are a little bit better in the particular course than he is.

Parents of high school students seem to believe that they are doing the students a favor by enrolling them in small classes in which there are very few students per teacher. This creates a sense of dependency in the academic work of the student. This dependency will disappear overnight when the student walks onto a college campus. Why parents should think that it is a good idea to have students become dependent upon the personal intervention of a teacher in a classroom is beyond me. The student who is advancing educationally should require less and less intervention by classroom teachers.

The tendency is for students to take advantage of any free ride that they can get. This is the tendency of anybody. This is why it is dangerous to have small classes in high school. It creates a sense of dependency that will weaken the student's ability to compete in college. To enroll a student into a class with a low student-teacher ratio is a real disservice to the student. The student walks onto a college campus and enrolls in a course were there may be as many as 1,000 students listening to a professor lecture. I mentioned this is the previous chapter. These are called mega classes, and they are cash cows for colleges. The course probably is broken up into discussion groups of about 30 students, which are monitored by graduate students with no teaching experience. Nothing prepares a high school senior for this kind of transition. It is one of the reasons why half of all college freshmen do not graduate.

There are probably high school or even college graduates reading this who would like to have some of these skills. There is no reason you could not sign up for the course on goal-setting, time management, and study habits. It's never too late.

10

WHAT COLLEGES WANT

What colleges want when they admit a freshman is almost the opposite of what parents want their children to be at the time of high school graduation. This has always been true, because what colleges want is a compliant student whose thinking can be reworked by the faculty. Colleges want to break a student's confidence in the moral, religious, and political outlook of parents rich enough to send their children to college to be brainwashed by a usually liberal faculty. This has been going on for a long time. Aristophanes wrote a comedy about it 2,300 years ago: *The Clouds*.

A college admissions office looks at such things as high school grades, extracurricular activities, and, above all, the SAT or ACT score. The SAT or ACT score lets the admissions office compare the performance of many applicants. The admissions office does not want to let anybody into the program who is likely to flunk out. It wants the highest score it can get, but at the same time, admissions officers know that the very best students are likely to go to a better college.

There is great competition for good students, but mostly it is competition for money from their parents and from the state legislature. Colleges are in a major financial bind. This is going to get a great deal worse, because, as I've mentioned, it is now possible for students to graduate from an accredited university for about $15,000 or less. Most tax-funded universities cost at least $15,000 a year: tuition, room, board, and textbooks. Some private universities cost three or four times this much. So when parents finally figure out that they do not have to dip into their retirement savings portfolio in order to send one child through college, let alone three, competition for students is going to increase.

———

Colleges want to get students enrolled as freshmen because this is where they make most of their money. It costs relatively little to teach freshmen or sophomores, yet the tuition payment is the same as for upper-division years. (The upper division is where the student majors in a particular subject. This is where he gets taught by PhD-holding professors rather than graduate assistants who have never had any training in teaching. The payoff in education for the student is in the upper division.) Therefore, colleges do their best to persuade parents and students that it is necessary to spend the first two years on campus. It is not necessary, either economically or academically. But it is not in the self-interest of colleges that families understand this.

It is a matter of public record that the first two years of

college impart almost no information to students. *There is no improvement in student performance for the freshman and sophomore years in college.*[1] This is an enormous failure on the part of colleges, but parents seem unaware of what statisticians have discovered. So do most students, who are victims of this system. Students unknowingly waste precious time, and their parents pay very high prices, when the first two years of college can be completed during high school, by means of CLEP exams and DSST exams, and for a total cost of about $2,000. The student can live at home, complete high school through online education, get a part-time job locally, pass the CLEP or DSST exams by using used, inexpensive older editions of college-level textbooks, and enter college as a junior. Most colleges hate this strategy, but this is the new reality. It is their problem, not the parents'.

———·•·———

Therefore, what we find is that parental interests and collegiate interests are opposed to each other. The only reason that parents consent to the traditional college scenario is that they do not know there are alternatives, not just at the college level, but also at the high school level. The student does not have to go through a lockstep program of high school classroom instruction in order to get into a good college. Furthermore,

---

1. Richard Arum and Josipa Roksa, *Academically Adrift: Limited Learning on College Campuses* (Chicago: University of Chicago Press, 2011). For a grim review of this book's findings, go here: http://bit.ly/LowerDivision.

because most students do not seek entrance into the top four dozen schools, the degrees they earn do not enable them to get any particular advantage in the marketplace. As long as a student has a bachelor's degree from an accredited college or university, his degree is worth approximately as much as any comparable degree from the vast majority of American colleges.

These days, a degree is not worth a great deal of money anyway. Over half of all students with college degrees wind up in jobs that do not require a college degree. Ever since 2008, the job market for college graduates has been a disaster. If a student has not majored in something such as petroleum engineering or another engineering degree, he is likely to wind up in a low-paying job whose requirements have nothing to do with his college major. Richard Vedder, an economist at Ohio University, offered this assessment in 2010: "Over 317,000 waiters and waitresses have college degrees (over 8,000 of them have doctoral or professional degrees), along with over 80,000 bartenders, and over 18,000 *parking lot attendants* [italics in the original]. All told, some 17,000,000 Americans with college degrees are doing jobs that the BLS [Bureau of Labor Statistics] says require less than the skill levels associated with a bachelor's degree."[2]

Colleges want bright students who already accept the basic outlook of the liberal arts faculty, which is politically liberal.

---

2. Richard Vedder, "Why Did 17 Million Students Go to College?" *Chronicle of Higher Education*, Oct. 20, 2010; see http://bit.ly/ VedderJobs.

They want students who can write well, think clearly, and parrot the party line of the classroom. In other words, they want intelligent students who conform to the outlook of the faculty.

Colleges want to deal with students who require no time outside the classroom. These students learn rapidly, pass their exams with high grades, and offer no challenge to the professor's views. Most important, their parents' checks never bounce. It is becoming more difficult to find students like these.

A growing number of colleges are therefore accepting students with homeschooling backgrounds rather than the standard classroom schooling dominant in the public schools and in most private schools. (That procedure produces students who are predictable, but not self-motivated, creative, or ready for upper-division work.). If the student has scored well on his SAT or ACT exam, or, even better from the point of view of the parents, has passed enough CLEP exams to let him enter as a sophomore or junior, he is going to get admission to most colleges. (Some colleges will not accept CLEP exams, precisely because the colleges make so much money in parking with virtually no education to students during the first two years. These students are seen as cash cows.) But competition is increasing, and enough colleges accept CLEP exams, so that those that do not are facing serious problems with recruiting. These problems are going to increase.

Students who received their education in a homeschool environment perform above average, and are well-prepared for college-level work. Colleges want the tuition checks from the parents, so they grant admission to these nontraditional students. The problem for the faculty members is that these students tend not to be conformists. They are more likely to have been trained with a set of presuppositions in opposition to those of the typical liberal arts college professor. Professors find it difficult to persuade students trained in a homeschool environment to change their views. The students are not impressed by classroom instruction. They have not been subjected to it. Their examination papers do not reflect the prevailing outlook of the public school curriculum. They have gained their educations outside the bureaucratic, textbook-based environment of the typical public school. But professors are usually happy to teach above-average students, even when those students do not share their views. There are so few students who show any degree of creativity or independent thought that college professors are usually overjoyed to have anybody in class who pays attention to what they say, even though the student may not agree with them.

I do not think it is a good idea to send students into a classroom environment in which their views are going to be discriminated against. There are better ways for students to get college degrees that do not require them to go through the ideological meat grinder represented by the typical liberal arts college. Students in upper-division courses are less likely to be pressured by faculty members, because those faculty members assume that the screening was done during the first two years of college. They assume that the students have already accepted the party line of higher education, so they are not as apt to be actively hostile to students who do not accept the party line. If a student can get into school as a junior, it is to his and the family's advantage.

———•—•———

There is some agreement between parents and colleges regarding the benefits of the student capable of performing college-level work. Colleges do not want to expel students. They do not want to waste their time teaching students who will not be able to graduate. If a student enters college capable of performing in a collegiate setting, the parents are happy and the college is happy. Student performance is the most important single criterion of success, and both parents and college authorities agree on this point.

Colleges do not provide much assistance to students who are not self-motivated. If a student has been nagged by his parents and his teachers to hand his work in on time, he is going to be in trouble when he hits college. There is nobody at college to nag him—unless he is a star athlete in an athletic scholarship program. A student who has survived high school only because he was nagged is not in a good position to survive on a college campus. Very few homeschooled students need this kind of nagging.

———•—•———

Colleges want bright students who accept the outlook of the liberal arts faculty. They also want parents to send checks that do not bounce. As competition has increased for these students, colleges have accepted more homeschooled students. If the students have passed the SAT or ACT with high marks, the colleges welcome them. There is no discrimination against homeschooled students who pass the entrance exams with good marks.

11

THE RON PAUL CURRICULUM

The most important aspect of any program of education is the curriculum. Whether it is delivered in the form of books, online articles, YouTube videos, recitations, essay writing, term paper writing, public speaking, or classroom lectures, it is the content of the curriculum that is central.

As I have argued throughout this book, parents have the authority—meaning the legitimate power—to determine the content of their children's education. They can delegate to specialists the actual instruction process. They have done this for thousands of years. There was a time when rich families hired tutors to educate their children in the home. As early as 1642, the Massachusetts Bay Colony passed a requirement that towns provide schools to educate children in the Bible. In 1837 the State of Massachusetts created a Department of Education, and from that time on, parents made the decision whether to send their children to a tax-funded school or to private school. Alternatively, parents could teach the children at home.

Parents cannot evade the responsibility of determining which curriculum best meets the needs of their children. The delegation of authority does not transfer authority away from the parents. It merely transfers the details of implementing that authority to a third party. But the third party answers to somebody—ultimately the parents or the state.

With the resurrection of homeschooling in America ever since the late 1970s, parents have regained control over the content of their children's education.[1] They have become more familiar with the books and materials available for family education. They have learned more about what works in terms of teaching students skills. But as the student gets older, and the materials get more complex and more difficult, parents again face the problem of delegating to third parties the responsibility for adopting a curriculum and a teaching methodology. Parents do not have great confidence in their own abilities once the child enters high school.

This is why parents must exercise great caution in deciding which curriculum to assign to their children. They may not be in a position to read all materials in the curriculum, but they should at least trust the person who has assembled it. This is why competing curriculum materials are based heavily on trust. Parents trust other homeschooling parents when making evaluations of specific curriculums. They talk with other parents on homeschooling forums. They attend homeschooling

---

1. Milton Gaither, *Homeschool: An American History* (New York: Palgrave Macmillan, 2008), chap. 6.

conventions, where they can hear presentations from sellers of curriculum materials. They do not turn over their children's education to third parties without a careful investigation of the competing claims of the sellers of the materials.

We are seeing a proliferation of homeschool materials. This is positive. Parents have far greater degrees of choice today than they had even a decade ago. They can find material that better matches their goals for their children, their children's abilities, and their presuppositions about the way the world works, or at least should work. The fit between the curriculum and the child is much better today than it was a decade ago, let alone a generation ago.

———•———

I believe a program should target students in the top 20 percent. In other words, 80 percent of the students presently enrolled in classroom environments in the United States should not be the targets of a homeschool program. The students who are targeted have to be self-disciplined. They have to be self-motivated. They should not be dependent on parental nagging to get them through the program. If the student is dependent upon parental nagging, the parent would be wise to choose a homeschool program other than the one I have put together.

By concentrating on the top 20 percent of students, I am concentrating on people who I expect to be leaders at some point in the future. *The entire curriculum is based on the development of leadership*. This has to be the top 20 percent of a cross section of kids who would otherwise be in a classroom. I am not trying to educate the top 1 percent. I am not even trying to educate the top 4 percent. The curriculum I have assembled is suitable for students in the top 4 percent, or even the top 1 percent, but they will get through it faster.

A homeschool curriculum, K–3, should be aimed at helping the teacher—presumably the mother but it could certainly be the father—impart the basics of self-learning to young children. The videos and other teaching materials are therefore aimed at an adult teacher, not at the student. But sometime around fourth grade, the educational program shifts in the direction of self-instruction. More and more of the work is done by the student. The best way to do this is to require a daily writing assignment. The student has got to learn how to analyze what is read, and then put the pieces together in the form of a simple essay. Students who write a weekly essay, or even a daily essay, learn the basics of analytical reasoning and writing before they reach high school. They begin to develop these skills quite early, but they become self-educated beginning about the sixth grade.

It is difficult to decide when to make the transition. Some students are ready in the fourth grade. Others are not ready until the fifth. Some students are ready only in the sixth grade. Because I am targeting the top 20 percent, the program I have designed aims at making the transition to self-education at the beginning of the fourth grade. The fourth grade is not entirely based on the principle of self-education, but it moves in that direction by the end of the year. Then, in the fifth grade, the student begins to accept greater responsibility for his own education. The curriculum is geared to helping a student make this transition.

With this in mind, I want to describe the curriculum that I have assembled. I want you to understand the logic of the curriculum, but I also want you to understand its technology.

One size does not fit all. Therefore, the ideal high school curriculum should have four tracks. There should be one track for students who want to specialize in the social sciences and humanities. There should be a second track for students who want to go into natural science. The third track should be aimed at students who want to apprentice with a local businessman in high school and then turn this experience into a career. The fourth track should be a fine arts track.[2] The student would make the decision in his second year of high school to take one or another of the tracks. This is the equivalent of deciding on a major in college.

My curriculum will concentrate initially on the social sciences and humanities. I think there is a greater market among my readers for this than for the other tracks, although the business track will also be popular. The curriculum will provide sufficient courses on mathematics and science to enable a

---

2. This is the hardest nut to crack. The fine arts require hands-on experience and a mentor.

graduate to get into a good college, if this is what the student wants to do. (Even better: earn a BA by distance learning at age eighteen.) A meaningful college course in physics requires the student to know calculus. This is why high school physics should be given in the senior year, and only to students who have already had at least one year of calculus. The kind of physics taught in the typical high school is not really the equivalent of a college-level physics class. So students have to understand calculus before they take physics. The earlier courses in science should be aimed at either earth science or biology. Students taking these sciences do not require an advanced math course to get a preliminary grounding. Chemistry falls somewhere in the middle.

With respect to starting a home-based business, my curriculum in the senior year is going to devote considerable time to the basics of running a business. Students interested in starting a business will be allowed to take courses in business math rather than calculus. They will be given training in how to write effective advertising copy. This will be part of their English class in the senior year. This is an aspect of rhetoric. Nothing like this is taught in any high school I am aware of. At the end of the student's sophomore year, he will be allowed to begin coursework in entrepreneurship. This is an aspect of business. Students going into business should have a more intense understanding of economic theory than those majoring in the natural sciences or the fine arts.

Public high schools over the last generation have abandoned the teaching of history. They have substituted what they call social studies, which is geared to contemporary politics such as global warming, poverty, multiculturalism, gender politics, and similar politically correct topics. People can major in these fields in college, but when they graduate, they are unemployable. I see no reason to substitute this kind of social science, which is basically contemporary politics, for a detailed study of Western civilization and American history.

This is why the curriculum that my staff is putting together requires each student to take two years of Western civilization. Colleges a generation ago required students to take a one-year course in Western civ, but very few colleges require this today. With my program, at the end of his junior year, a student will have a better understanding of the history of Western civilization than 95 percent of all college graduates in the United States. If parents think this is an advantage, they will adopt my curriculum.

This curriculum uses a teaching strategy not used in any high school and only by a handful of expensive private colleges. The curriculum is self-reinforcing. When the student takes the Western civilization course, he also takes a course in Western literature. So in his history course the student reads about the history of a particular civilization in a particular time period, and in his English course he reads representative examples of the literature of that society in that same period. The student learns to recognize those aspects of the literature of a particular culture as manifesting the presuppositions that undergirded the entire society.

This way, a student begins to understand the interrelationship of literature, politics, religion, economics, family life, and civil justice. He sees that there are connections among all these aspects of social life. He is able to assess these interrelationships. The course in history will not be pure abstraction. It will be reinforced by examples that provide evidence that a particular worldview of a particular society in a particular era was manifested in the literature of that era.

It is common in English classes for the English teacher, who majored in English, to teach literature in terms of the academic criteria of English departments. The teacher focuses on plot, mood, tone, and a lot of concepts understood only by people who majored in English. The typical student is not going to major in English; nor is he particularly interested in the subtleties of literary creation, let alone literary criticism. He is interested in the plot insofar as it holds his attention. If it does not hold his attention, he is not interested in plot. Then he is surely uninterested in the techniques that the author used to create the plot.

The importance of literature in society can be very great. But its importance must be assessed in terms of the widely held presuppositions of the people in that society regarding the five major points of social theory: God, man, law, causation, and time. To the extent that a piece of literature illustrates one or more of these fundamental categories of social theory, the student benefits from a careful reading of that piece of literature. He is able to fit this information into an overall perspective of what a particular society in a particular period held as its fundamental tenets of faith.

At the end of the two-year course in Western civilization, a student should have a good understanding of the changes that have taken place in the thinking of large numbers of people in the West. Modern society is certainly not a complex mirror image of Greek society in 300 B.C. Christianity has shaped the development of Western civilization. So has the Enlightenment. There been many competing worldviews in the history of Western civilization, and different cultures in the West have adopted different aspects of these competing worldviews. A student at the end of this course will have a good understanding of how the various beliefs that were promoted by specific religions and movements have infiltrated modern society and yet have been modified by rival positions.

My goal is to equip the student to be a good citizen, but more than this, to be a productive member of a society that is not fundamentally political. Greek society in 300 B.C. was overwhelmingly political. So was Roman society. But this was not true of the Hebrews; nor was it true of the early church. Of far greater importance were the family, the ecclesiastical hierarchy, economics, and land ownership.

In addition to courses in Western literature and in Western history, there will be courses in economics and government. Then there will be a one-year course in American history, which will be paralleled by a one-year course in the U.S. Constitution. I want students to have a detailed familiarity with the Constitution, and with the political developments in Supreme Court decisions that have replaced the original intent of the framers of the Constitution and the voters who ratified it.

My curriculum will inoculate the student against the

Keynesianism of the typical university. He will not enter college intellectually unarmed. He will have a good understanding of the history of the United States, the history of Western civilization, the development of literature, economic development, and the growth of the welfare-warfare state. He will know the weaknesses of government intervention into the economy. He will not be taken in by the standard textbook accounts of Franklin Roosevelt's New Deal. He will have been given a thorough introduction to the libertarian principle of nonintervention: the freedom philosophy of peace and prosperity. He will not only know the theory of nonintervention, but will be familiar with the outcomes of repeated violations of the principle of nonintervention by the federal government.

———•·•———

It is not good enough to be aware of the history of Western civilization and the United States, including constitutional development. The student must also be able to express himself effectively. This requires weekly writing assignments. These writing assignments will begin in the fourth grade. By the time the student reaches high school, he will be able to express himself on paper and on-screen. Second, there will be considerable attention given to public speaking. Even though mine is an online curriculum, students will get training in public speaking. For every course, he will be required to post videos on their own YouTube channels. Each will be required to set up a blog, either on Blogger or WordPress.

In other words, the student will become familiar with the techniques and technology of communication and persuasion. This is extremely important for students who go into business, or who expect to have influence locally in the community. A student who can write clearly and rapidly, outline a speech, and deliver it in front of an audience has a tremendous competitive advantage over almost every high school graduate, and the vast majority of college graduates.

One aspect of my curriculum has a ninth-grade focus. There will be a course on time management, goal-setting, and study habits. There will be another course on fundamentals of leadership. All students will be required to take these courses when they begin high school. There are courses on speed-reading and typing. Students will be encouraged to continue with these two courses throughout their careers. If a student can type rapidly and accurately, and read rapidly and accurately, he will have a tremendous advantage over the vast majority of Americans.

My goal is to add a high school year every eight months. I will add a year upward, and I will also add years at the bottom. I plan to offer courses on how to teach young children to read and write. These courses will be offered free of charge to the general public. In fact, the entire curriculum will be free of charge up until the sixth grade. I want to make certain that my site provides basic education to any family, anywhere in the world. I want to maximize the number of people who benefit from this program. This is going to take several years to develop, but that is my goal for kindergarten through fifth grade education.

At the high school level, things get more rigorous. At that level, the site will be closed to the general public. Only paying families will gain access to it. I want to train a generation of leaders, and I intend to do so by means of a rigorous curriculum that rests on the freedom philosophy. It is a philosophy of *self-government*.

So far, I have discussed the content of the curriculum. Now I want to talk about the technology.

———•◦•———

Some students need audio instruction. To give them this, each high school class will make use of video screencasts. A screencast integrates a presentation program such as PowerPoint with audio instruction. The student can follow each presentation by means of an outline, and the instructor fills in the outline by means of a lecture. Each screencast will be about twenty-five minutes. Then there will be a reading assignment, generally in primary sources in history, but also tied to extracts from Wikipedia and summaries of textbooks.

The courses will have a "four-one" structure: four lessons will present new material, and one lesson will review that material. This way, the student is forced to go back over material that has already been covered, because otherwise he will not remember much of it.

There will be a weekly writing assignment for each course, on the fifth day of the weekly presentation. Presumably, this will be a Friday for most students. Students will watch a summary screencast of the week's four lessons, and then will write a 250-word paper. This is for each course. If students do not get this done on Friday, then they will have to work on Saturday to do it.

Students will begin training in public speaking. They will be required to prepare short videos to be posted to their YouTube channels. The student will verbally summarize what he wrote in an essay for another course. He will not read the essay; he will summarize it, so that someone who has not read it will have a good overall understanding of what is said in it.

Because students will be required to post their essays on their blogs, and to post their videos on their YouTube channels, they will feel the pressure to do a good job. Students do not want to go public without preparation. In the early years, this is going to take a lot of extra time.

Most of us know that the best way to learn something new is to teach it. So students will be encouraged to interact with one another on forums for each of their courses. If a student cannot figure something out, he can go online and ask for assistance. Other students will respond to his questions by preparing a screencast and posting it on their YouTube channels and then posting a link to it on the forum. This will enable students to develop their teaching skills.

I would like to see students in the natural sciences and mathematics create blogs that will include lists of frequently asked questions. They can create videos that will help other students get these questions answered.

Students' blogs and YouTube channels can be used to deal with any truant officer who might insist on evidence that the student is actually learning something. Truant officers are not used to seeing comprehensive websites by students, backed up by videos posted on the students' YouTube channels.

If a student develops a blog with hundreds of pages of essays, plus links to videos, he will have a tremendous asset when it comes time to go looking for a job. How many job applicants have this kind of publicly available evidence of their competence? An employer will know that the student is capable in the two crucial areas: written communication and verbal communication. He will also know that the student is capable technically with two of the most important means of communication, namely, YouTube videos and blogs. The student will go to the top of the pile of job applicants.

Parents will be able to see an improvement in their children's ability to write and appear in educational videos. The ability to pass true-false exams does not give students a particular advantage after graduation. In contrast, the ability to write an essay and then produce an instructional video is highly sought after in the field of business.

———•◦•———

My curriculum is organized in terms of these assumptions:

1. A curriculum must be integrated and coherent.
2. There must be a common theme: the freedom philosophy.
3. The best methodology is self-instruction.
4. Courses should reinforce each other.
5. Students must learn to write and to speak in public.

If this sounds like something you would be interested in as an adult, you should consider signing up as a student. You will get the education you deserved when you were a teenager, but that was not available at the time. You will also be able to interact with your children, if they are being instructed by means of my curriculum. Most adults probably will not want to go through all the courses, but some of them will be interesting, especially the course on leadership, and maybe the course on how to start a small business, as well as courses in basic economics. Some adults will want to take the history courses, too.

If you are interested in learning more about this program, send an email to:

paulcurriculum@aweber.com

———•◦•———

Here are some things to remember from part 3:

Maybe you are a parent of a teenager. If so, you are concerned about the content and structure of the education your child is receiving.

If you are a homeschool parent, you know there is a wide variety of curriculum materials out there, and they vary in quality considerably, from course to course. You want your child to have the best materials available, but the materials have got to be interesting enough to get your child to commit to mastering them. The materials should not be too far over your child's head. You also do not want them to be so easy that your child gains no skill in mastering more difficult material. You want to prepare your child for life, and for college. You want your child to be ready to walk onto a college campus and not get ground up by the Keynesian liberalism that is dominant on the campus.

In other words, you want to do a responsible job when selecting a curriculum for your children. You have to act on their behalf. You may be interested at this point in learning about the curriculum I am putting together. It may be exactly what you have been looking for. On the other hand, it may not be. You do not know yet, but you are in a position to find out.

Maybe you do not have children still in school. Maybe you are a grandparent, and your grandchildren are already in school or will be in a few years. You may want to find out more about my curriculum, or about other online programs.

What I am proposing will not work well where children are not self-disciplined. They also had better be future-oriented. But they do not have to have high IQs. They do have to have a commitment to overcoming challenges. They must also be able to overcome the usual temptations we all face, but that teenagers especially face. It is easy to take ethical shortcuts. It is easy to quit. It is easy to complain endlessly until somebody over us finally tells us to quit.

A self-disciplined teenager will probably be a self-disciplined adult. Someone who is future-oriented when he is a teenager will probably be future-oriented when he is an adult. When he learns the basics of self-education, a teenager is in a position to advance his career and also advance his calling in ways that his contemporaries are not. If a teenager has a sense of the battle of ideas we are in today, and he is willing to make an initial commitment to enter that battle as an ideological warrior, he is likely to make contributions on some ideological battlefield over the next sixty or seventy years. The world will be better off because of his contributions.

This is a win-win situation. Parents do not have to bankrupt themselves for a college education that can be purchased a lot cheaper than the general public suspects. Their children are immunized early against the Keynesian liberalism of the modern university. Maybe the children do not even set foot on the university campus. They can still earn an accredited degree that would grant them the same benefits as the majority of college degrees.

A teenager who gets involved in a program like this is going to have an enormous head start over his peers. His peers may be as smart, and they may even be equally self-disciplined academically, but they are not going to be exposed to a curriculum that is as internally consistent, focused on the history of Western civilization, dedicated to the principle of restricting the state, equally dedicated to the principle of self-government, and taught by experts.

Smart students are going to be successful if they are ethically grounded. They will do well, no matter which curriculum they use. This is why the ethical environment of the educational program is so important. Very smart students can find themselves in an ethical crisis, and their brains may not get them out of it. We are warned from an early age that "if you lie down with dogs, you get up with fleas."

Parents who control their children's educational environment are in a much stronger position to increase the likelihood of their children's academic success than parents who turn their children over to a school system seeking to satisfy the state's Department of Public Instruction. The moral environment is far more important than the academic environment. But parents are in a position today to get both: a reliable moral environment and a superior academic program. This is because they can keep their children home and assign homeschool materials to them. If they get these materials online, the costs are reasonable. If their children use CLEP and DSST exams to test out of the first two years of college before they graduate from high school, the parents will be so far ahead of the curve financially that the expenses associated with homeschooling will be chump change by comparison.

Parents will be ahead, and the students will also be ahead. The students will graduate from college at least two years early, thereby getting into the labor force two years earlier. Not every student who signs up for my curriculum will be able to do this. I think a lot of them can, and at least they will be encouraged to try.

There will be far more choices in a decade than there are today. The number of comprehensive curriculum programs will multiply. As more students who have been homeschooled go into the production of homeschool materials, there is going to be a flood of high-quality materials. We are only in the initial stages of an educational revolution. The best is yet to come.

But that will be then, and this is now. What are you going to do now? What is best for your children and grandchildren now? What is the best deal you can get immediately on a curriculum you approve of?

My program is in the initial phase. I do not know when you are reading this. The program will expand year by year from the ninth grade through the twelfth. It will also expand upward, from kindergarten through the ninth grade. It is going to take some years to finish the program, but it is coming.

If you know somebody who might be helped, loan out a copy of this book. Ask to get it back in a week. Tell the borrower that you will be happy to talk about it. This book may offer an immediate solution to somebody who is facing a major problem in educating his teenagers. This book could be a lifesaver for some parent. It could also be a lifesaver for some student. Lend it out, get it back, and lend it out again.

CONCLUSION

You have arrived at the end. Thank you for sticking with me this far. An author always knows that not all the readers who s tart his book will finish it. Sad, but true. Listeners usually do not walk out during someone's speech. But readers put down a book never to pick it up again.

I don't know if you have already made the transition to homeschooling. If you have, then I have been preaching to the choir. That's okay. Choirs need a good sermon every so often. If every chapter is a sermon, you have heard several.

On the other hand, you may be on the fence. You are not sure if you are ready to switch from the convenience of tax-funded schools. (They *are* convenient... until a school-based disaster strikes a family.)

I have probably lost those parents who are convinced that they, as individuals, can somehow get together with like-minded parents to reform the local public schools. Parents have been attempting this since about 1840. This strategy has not worked well. In recent decades, it has not worked at all.

By now, you know the major themes of this book. Some are negative. Most are positive.

With respect to the negative themes, there is this: tax-funded education has been corrupted by money from on high, state and federal money. Federal money always brings federal control. State money has the same effect on local school districts: loss of local control, meaning centralization. Funding always identifies the locus of sovereignty in any organization. Follow the money. It leads back to Washington, DC.

Second, there has been a measurable decline in the performance of tax-funded schools. This began long before I entered school, but it has accelerated ever since the mid-1960s. This decline has not been limited to academics. The moral environment has also decayed. Safety has declined. Yet the cost per student has risen relentlessly, adjusted for inflation. In 1961 the average cost in year 2000 dollars was around $2,800. In 2008 it was close to $11,000.[3]

This decline is becoming visible to more and more people, especially parents. Voters are beginning to figure out they do not live in Lake Wobegon. All the local schools are not above average. Worse, the average is declining. The lowest common denominator keeps getting lower.

When we look at the big picture, we may be tempted to de-

---

3. "Expenditures," *Fast Facts*, National Center for Education Statistics, 2012; see 1.usa.gov/1uRf7V.

spair. There has been educational reform after reform for over a century. None has worked. Each reform is abandoned as a fad. But none of them was called a fad by the reformers when it was introduced. The reforms become fads only in retrospect. Example: the "new math" fad of the late 1960s. I'll tell you some people who learned the new math well: congressmen. The trouble is, Congress has yet to abandon new math. The schools did forty years ago.

The big picture is like an iceberg. All the local critic has is a blowtorch.

This leads me to the other major themes of this book. They are positive. They are positive because of the little picture. The little picture is *your* picture. You have the authority to veto the public school system inside the four walls of your home. You do not have to cooperate any longer.

The phrase "vote with your feet" was applied for decades to people who escaped from Soviet nations. The border guards tried to prevent this form of voting.

In Germany today, it is illegal to homeschool your children. Across Europe it is illegal. The bureaucrats inside the schools have persuaded the politicians to make voting with your children's feet illegal. This is not true in the United States. Yes, there are government restrictions on homeschools. There are petty interferences with parental sovereignty. But this is not Germany. There are ways to take your children out of traditional schools and keep them out.

The cost of doing this keeps dropping. Salman Khan's Khan Academy teaches students around the world free of charge. Others will imitate him. There is a flood of homeschool materials today, not the trickle of 1980. There is a wide range of choice, and this will grow wider. The economist says, "When the price falls, more is demanded." Demand is rising fast.

Adam Smith taught a unique doctrine in his day. He said that when individuals pursue their self-interest in an open economy, they create wealth. This wealth benefits the entire society. He described this in *The Wealth of Nations*. He called for the removal of restrictions on free men's decisions to seek what they believe is best for themselves and their families.

The same argument applies to privately funded education. When parents become buyers of educational services in a free market, they do so in the name of their children. By turning to the free market for solutions to their problems in gaining the educational training they want for their children, they benefit society. They promote competition among producers of educational programs. The supply then increases. The division of labor increases. Output increases. The range of choices increases.

The departure of a child from a tax-funded school sends a message to local public school administrators: "Improve the schools or suffer negative consequences." For every child who is removed, the local district loses funding from the state. This pressures administrators to cut costs. It pressures them to try a new reform.

As surely as sending an e-mail pressures the U.S. Postal Service to cut costs, so does the departure of a student from a local school. Parents get the educational program they want for their children. As a side effect, this pressures local administrators to fix the system. If the administrators refuse, then other parents will get the message.

———•••———

Malcolm Gladwell wrote a bestselling book titled *The Tipping Point*. I especially like its subtitle: *How Little Things Can Make a Big Difference*. It was published in 2000. That book has made a big difference, and a lot of money, too. The book rests on a line of reasoning that is not intuitive. Gladwell describes major social changes as epidemics. They have the characteristic features of epidemics. He identifies the three characteristic features: contagion, small causes, and the transition from gradual change to a dramatic moment when everything seems to change all at once. This is a powerful metaphor. But it has a glaring defect. Epidemics recede rapidly. Social changes sometimes do, but sometimes they don't. They can take hold of a society, for good or ill. They can become permanent.

The homeschooling movement is small but dedicated. The public schools are fat and complacent. It looks as though the idea of tax-funded education is permanent. The exodus from the schools is minimal. But this David versus Goliath situation can be reversed. I believe it will be reversed. When Washington's checks bounce, it will be reversed.

A generation ago, a very fine American historian named Clarence Carson wrote a book, *The World in the Grip of an Idea*. That idea was socialism. The book was published in

1979. It argued that the whole world was being influenced by individuals who believed in socialism. The idea was spreading. It is not spreading today. It has retreated from the public arena.

In 1996, Carson wrote an article that looked back on that book published a dozen years before the fall of the USSR in 1991. He admitted that the fall of the Soviet Union was a major setback for socialists of all varieties. In my view, it was more than a major setback. It was an unexpected event that undermined the very word *socialism*. In short, it was a tipping point. There is Keynesianism today. It is the preferred system for government intervention for every country outside of North Korea. But this is not socialism: the state's ownership of the means of production. It is the same old welfare state dressed up in formulas and jargon. But I agree with Carson's closing words:

The idea that has the world in its grip has great attraction for peoples around the world. The notion that government is responsible for the material and intellectual well-being of populaces has great appeal, especially when it is accompanied by actual payments and subsidies from government. Many people become dependent upon government handouts, and even those who are not particularly dependent may lose confidence in their ability to provide for themselves. These feelings, attitudes, and practices are residues from the better part of a century of socialism in its several varieties. They have produced vastly overgrown governments and the politicalization of life. Governments and politicians are the problem, not the solution.

Sturdy individuals, stable families, vital communities, limited government, and faith in a transcendent God who provides for us through the natural order and the bounties of nature—these alone can break the grip of the idea. It is now a cliché that socialism is a failure; it now is the fullness of time to act upon the insight that gave rise to its fall.[4]

I believe that family-run, family-funded education is an important component of any program of anti-Keynesian reform. It starts small, the way that Gladwell says an epidemic starts. It starts with you. As Leonard E. Read always said, reform must begin with us. The most effective way to reform the tax-funded schools is for dedicated parents to remove their children from those schools. The only way to persuade a senior bureaucrat to reform his bureaucracy is to reduce its funding. Every time a child is removed from a local school, the district loses state funding. That catches the bureaucrats' attention. The more often it happens, the more it catches their attention.

This does not require any political action. It does not require mobilization of any kind. It does not succeed or fail based on voters showing up at the polls. All it takes is parents deciding to bring their children home. No more yellow buses.

---

4. Clarence Carson, "The World in the Grip of an Idea Revisited," *The Freeman* (May 1, 1996); see http://tinyurl.com/WeakenedGrip.

No more peer pressure for fashion updates. No more PTA meetings. No more parent-teacher conferences. Just a desk; some inexpensive supplies; maybe a few textbooks, or maybe none, if the program is entirely digital and online, the way mine is. (With my curriculum, all the books the students use are printed out, with only one exception in kindergarten, and one in high school: Hayek's *Road to Serfdom*. It's a paperback.)

—————

I am well aware of just how big a commitment this is. It will change the way parents interact with their children. Parents can no longer be spectators who talk briefly with their children during unscheduled moments in between school, TV, YouTube, texting, and Skype. I am assuming that you would like to speak with your children about important matters before the day the person at the college dorm desk hands the room key over to your last child to leave home.

Let's consider a few of the costs.

Time: A parent (usually the mother) must spend several hours a day with young children to help them with schoolwork. But with a well-designed curriculum that rests on a strategy of self-teaching and student tutorials, this time declines steadily after grade three. As children get older, they can and should teach themselves. By high school, the curriculum should be 98 percent self-taught. The parent's main task is to read writing assignments. The rest of it is taken care of.

Money: The costs are mostly textbook costs. If you can avoid textbooks by relying on public domain materials online, you can eliminate this expense. If you use an online curriculum, the costs are mainly paper and toner. A well-designed curriculum does not require physical textbooks.

Some programs are 100 percent free. Salman Khan's program is not complete, but he offers free math videos. My curriculum, when completed (target date: early 2015), will be free through the fifth grade. Kindergarten and third grade are available now. This gets families started. After fifth grade, it costs about what a textbook-based curriculum does. If you shop around, you can find online materials that are free or close to it.

Then there is forfeited income. If the mother is in the workforce, she will have to quit her job. Or if she is the major breadwinner, the father will have to quit. But don't forget to deduct the costs of participation in the workplace: taxes, child-care costs, commuting costs (time and car maintenance), wardrobe costs, food costs, and a whole host of others. There is also workplace pressure. There is the corporate rat race. All this gets left behind in the name of spending far more time raising and teaching your children.

Paperwork: Most states require homeschooling parents to keep records of what their children have studied. This is minimal. If you have your children do simple writing from at least the second grade, plus arithmetic worksheets, that is plenty. I recommend that homeschool families join the Home School Legal Defense Association. It supplies lawyers in a crisis. Local school districts like to avoid dealing with an HSLDA lawyer.

Frustration: From time to time, homeschool teachers hit an emotional brick wall. On a bad day, the teacher thinks she is not qualified, that nothing seems to work. But this is true of every job. I surely had days like that in my twenty-three years in Congress. But the next day will be better. Things get rolling again.

Peer Pressure: It is not just students who suffer from peer pressure. It is also their parents. Friends, relatives, and colleagues who still trust the local tax-funded schools find many reasons to dismiss homeschooling. It is just too radical. It breaks with the community.

They ask questions. "What about social skills?" Answer: "You mean like turning down drug dealers politely?" "What about sports?" Answer: "There are community sports leagues." "What about cheerleading or other activities?" Answer: "My daughter prefers community service and her part-time job, which pays for her college courses." "What college courses?" Answer: "CLEP exams." "What are CLEP exams?" Answer: "They are exams administered by the College Board, which also administers SAT exams. For ninety dollars a high school student can test out of a semester in college—maybe even two semesters. She wants to earn her BA from an accredited college on the day she graduates from high school. The whole deal costs about fifteen thousand dollars. Her part-time job pays for it. It costs about eleven dollars a day. So we don't have to pay for her college. Just search Google for 'college' and '$11.'"

That usually ends the peer pressure.

I have already mentioned the benefit of getting out of the corporate rat race, but here are many others.

Satisfaction: The parents who become responsible for something as important as the education of their children can see progress. This progress is measurable. Test scores rise. Reading skills increase. Writing skills increase. Arithmetic skills increase.

The parents know that they are in charge. This is satisfying. They know that their child is not dependent on a teacher in a classroom full of students, using textbooks written by strangers and screened by committees. The parents decide what their children should read. They monitor their performance. They are focused on their children, unlike a classroom teacher, whose attention is diverted by children with learning difficulties or behavior problems.

Safety: The concept of safety is broad. It encompasses physical safety, but far more important is moral safety. The older the children are, the more important this is. You can do a Google search for articles on the moral environment of children in middle schools. I did such a search. The older you are, the more it will amaze you.

Then there is ideological safety. What ideas govern the curriculum in your local schools? Not many parents know. Not many take the time to skim through the textbooks. They assume that everything is all right. But why should anyone assume this? Why should textbook writers, who are the product of today's universities, be reliable ideologically?

There is also psychological safety. Peer group pressure is intense. If a young person becomes the target of bullying, this can make the child's life miserable. The stories are continual. The U.S. National Institutes of Health did a study of this in 2009. Here is its summary: "Prevalence rates of having bullied others or having been bullied at school for at least once in the last 2 months were 20.8% physically, 53.6% verbally, 51.4% socially, or 13.6% electronically. Boys were more involved in physical or verbal bullying, whereas girls were more involved in relational bullying. Boys were more likely to be cyber bullies, whereas girls were more likely to be cyber victims."[5] The Canadian government has issued a pamphlet on this: *Bullying: We Can All Help Stop It*. Canada? Where there is supposedly racial and cultural harmony? Where things seem so calm? Yes. This is an international problem in tax-funded schools.

Then there is the security issue of the latchkey child. Parents who are absent during the day must deal with this problem. Children after school and during summers are unattended for several hours a day. This is not good for younger children or teenagers.

All these threats end on the day parents pull their child out of a local tax-funded school.

Student Performance: Tests show that homeschooled students perform above grade level. Just Google "homeschool test scores." The scores are way above norm. In a 2010 article on the debate over test scores, we read this: "Homeschooled students score about 72 points higher than the national average on the Scholastic Aptitude Test (SAT). The average American College Test (ACT) score is 21. The average score for homeschoolers is 22.8 out of a possible 36 points. Homeschoolers are at the 77th percentile on the Iowa Test of Basic Skills." The article cites a

---

5. *School Bullying among Adolescents in the United States: Physical, Verbal, Relational, and Cyber*; see http://tinyurl.com/BullyingNIH.

study made by a professor at Northeastern State University that stated "homeschoolers are more likely to come from homes with educated parents and higher incomes. Homeschooling parents are less likely to divorce (which is true of higher income couples in general). Homeschooled kids watch less television. All of this results in higher academic achievement."[6]

Wait a minute! Here is a study that says that students perform better in home-based schools because the home environment is so much better than in tax-funded schools. Is this supposed to persuade parents to leave their children in tax-funded schools that are not performing well? Are parents supposed to sacrifice their children's academic performance on the altar of political correctness?

In Congress, parents don't do this. If they live in the Washington, DC, school district, they usually send their children to private schools. Everyone on Capitol Hill knows this, but no one talks about it. The following report is from the Heritage Foundation. It reports on private school decisions made by senators and congressmen. Note: this includes those who live in upscale counties in Virginia and Maryland, which is a majority of congressmen. The report did not ask about those who lived inside the District of Columbia. Also note: only about 10 percent of Americans sent their children to private schools in 2009.[7]

---

6. "Do Homeschool Kids Really Rate Better on Standardized Tests?"; see http://tinyurl.com/HStestDebate.
7. "Enrollment Trends," *Fast Facts*, National Center for Educational Statistics, 2012; see http://tinyurl.com/Private2009.

- Forty-four percent of senators and 36 percent of representatives had at one time sent their children to private school.
- Twenty-three percent of House Education and Labor Committee members and nearly 40 percent of Senate Health, Education, Labor, and Pensions Committee members have ever sent their children to private school.
- Thirty-eight percent of House Appropriations Committee members and 35 percent of Senate Finance Committee members have ever sent their children to private school.
- Thirty-five percent of Congressional Black Caucus members and 31 percent of Congressional Hispanic Caucus members exercised private-school choice.[8]

It would be beneficial if they preached what they practiced, as Charles Murray so aptly puts it.[9]

Homeschooling parents can pay to have their children tested annually. The three main tests are the Stanford 10 Achievement Test, the Iowa Test of Basic Skills, and the California Achievement Test.

Self-Disciplined Children: If the curriculum that parents adopt stresses self-teaching, the students learn how to follow through on their own. This is a crucial skill, whether a student goes to work or to college after high school. This skill must be taught to most children.

---

8. "How Members of the 111th Congress Practice Private School Choice," April 20, 2009; see http://tinyurl.com/CongressmenChoose.
9. Charles Murray, *Coming Apart: The State of White America, 1960–2010* (New York: Crown Forum, 2012), p. 305.

Parents should guide young children, but at some point the parent should begin to transfer responsibility to the child. Nagging is a self-defeating practice. The high school graduate who needs to be nagged by a parent is in serious trouble. He should know how to complete tasks without intervention from others. He should know how to research topics on his own.

The curriculum should teach children how to learn. If it is online, it should provide tutorial opportunities. The best way to learn anything new is to teach it, once you have the rudiments mastered.

Parents say they are training their children to be independent. But when should this training begin? I think it should begin no later than the fifth grade. Students should be given more authority to teach themselves. This benefits the students. It also reduces the teaching time required for the parent-teacher.

————•••————

The educrats deeply resent homeschooling, but it is too late for them to roll it back. They tried this in the mid-1980s and failed. Politicians do not take on well-organized voter blocs that can inflict damage on them. Only if there is a stronger voting bloc pushing for a piece of legislation will politicians challenge a well-organized voting bloc.

Homeschoolers are digitally well connected. They are fanatical about defending their rights. They organize protests. They call legislators. They also cannot easily be monitored or policed. So the costs of enforcement are high, the political payoff is low, the risk of an organized response is high, and nobody in the general public really cares. At this point, it is way too late for politicians to stamp out homeschooling.

As more homeschooled children become adults and get the vote, it will be even riskier to take on the movement—and it is a movement. The numbers are growing. The success of homeschooled children in the National Spelling Bee and the National Geography Bee is well known by now. The test scores of homeschooled children are way above the norm. It is hard for school districts to impose sanctions on homeschool families. Local judges want evidence that the children are being cheated educationally. The evidence shows the contrary. The homeschooled children outperform public school children. The local school districts do not want a lawyer to bring this information out in court. It would be bad publicity.

This means that time is on the side of the homeschool movement. The court battles of the 1980s went against the educational establishment. Its attitude today is to let this sleeping dog lie. They do not want another series of court defeats.

The free market is a more powerful force than bureaucracy. The benefits that the free market provides are ever growing. The state cannot keep up with this, despite the power of coercion. Here we see a system that costs local communities over $10,000 per student per year. This system cannot match the output of a homeschool, where the costs of materials are under $500 a year. In the case of the Robinson Curriculum, one example of a homeschooling package available, it's $200, once per family, plus paper and toner.

When you can spend less and get a better product, the state goes on the defensive. Think of the U.S. Postal Service. There was no political movement behind the shrinking of the Postal Service. There was simply e-mail. One person at a time, Americans walked away from the USPS. They will never come back.

———•——

If you see that the benefits for your children will outweigh the costs borne by you as a parent-teacher, it is time to begin investigating homeschooling. Attend a convention. Link up with a homeschool group in your zip code. Look online for curriculum materials.

You will find that there are more choices than you have time to research thoroughly. It is not 1985 any longer.

One size doesn't fit all.

There are many sizes available today.

SOME OF MY FAVORITE WEBSITES

CampaignforLiberty.com

LewRockwell.com

Mises.org

RonPaulChannel.com

RonPaulCurriculum.com

RonPaulInstitute.org

RonPaulMD.com

TeaPartyEconomist.com

TomWoods.com